The Lancastria Tragedy

The Lancastria Tragedy

Stephen Wynn

PEN & SWORD
HISTORY
AN IMPRINT OF PEN & SWORD BOOKS LTD.
YORKSHIRE – PHILADELPHIA

First published in Great Britain in 2020 and reprinted in 2021 by
Pen & Sword Military
An imprint of
Pen & Sword Books Ltd
Yorkshire – Philadelphia

ISBN 978 1 52670 6 638

A CIP catalogue record for this book is
available from the British Library.

Printed and bound in the UK on FSC accredited paper by
4edge Ltd, Essex, SS5 4AD

Pen & Sword Books Limited incorporates the imprints of Atlas,
Archaeology, Aviation, Discovery, Family History, Fiction, History,
Maritime, Military, Military Classics, Politics, Select, Transport, True Crime,
Air World, Frontline Publishing, Leo Cooper, Remember When, Seaforth
Publishing, The Praetorian Press, Wharncliffe Local History, Wharncliffe
Transport, Wharncliffe True Crime and White Owl.

For a complete list of Pen & Sword titles please contact

PEN & SWORD BOOKS LIMITED
47 Church Street, Barnsley, South Yorkshire, S70 2AS, England
E-mail: enquiries@pen-and-sword.co.uk
Website: www.pen-and-sword.co.uk

Or

PEN AND SWORD BOOKS
1950 Lawrence Rd, Havertown, PA 19083, USA
E-mail: Uspen-and-sword@casematepublishers.com
Website: www.penandswordbooks.com

Contents

Introduction

This book is about the sinking of the HMT *Lancastria* on 17 June 1940 by aircraft of the German Luftwaffe and the subsequent cover-up ordered by the then British Prime Minister, Winston Churchill.

We will look at personal accounts from relatives of those who were on board the *Lancastria* when it was sunk. Some of these men survived whilst others were not so fortunate. It includes the *Lancastria*'s own history as a pre-war ocean-going liner through to its sinking off the west coast of France at St Nazaire.

The story has always centred on the number of those who perished that day; the number of those who survived is not open to question and has always been known. What will never be known is exactly how many people died when the *Lancastria* capsized and then sank after being struck by bombs dropped by aircraft of the Luftwaffe. The reason why the true figure will never be known is simple – nobody knows exactly how many people were on board the ship. The counting of those embarking, if it was ever actually begun, would have stopped long before the *Lancastria* was sunk, as it would quickly have been realised there was little or no point in it. The time taken to record everybody's name, rank, service number and regiment or corps, would have been too time consuming and have served no purpose. What would be the point of saying there were so many thousands of people on board the vessel before it was struck by the German bombs, without knowing who they were.

The sad thing is that those who had made it out to the *Lancastria* would have been feeling relieved in the knowledge that once they got underway, it was just a short journey cross the English Channel and the safety of finally being home.

I will also look at the reasons behind why Winston Churchill applied for a D-Notice restriction, preventing news of the day's events being revealed in the Press. In his memoirs Churchill later revealed that the reason he took the decision to keep the sinking of the *Lancastria* a secret from the public, was so as not to affect morale by bombarding them with more bad news. But was that the real reason why Churchill applied for the D-Notice? I don't think it was and I will explore that aspect in the book.

CHAPTER 1

The Birth of a Legend

The *Lancastria* did not begin her life with that name. Launched in 1920 she undertook her maiden voyage from Glasgow to Quebec on 19 June 1922 as the Royal Mail Steamship (RMS) *Tyrrhenia*. She had been built on the River Clyde for the Anchor Line, a subsidiary of the more famous Cunard Line.

The *Tyrrhenia* was 578 feet in length, weighed in excess of 16,000 gross tons and could carry 2,200 passengers, who were accommodated in three separate classes. In 1924 she was taken out of service to be refitted and in her new guise she catered for just two classes of passengers and not three as she had done previously. A slightly humorous aspect of the refurbishment was that the name of the ship was also changed at this time to the *Lancastria*. The humour comes in the reason for the change – passengers complained to the owners that they struggled to pronounce the ship's name. I do not know how the *Lancastria* came to be chosen as the ship's new name.

Once back in the water she took on a new route, this time sailing across the unpredictable waters of the Atlantic en route from Liverpool to New York and back again. The *Lancastria* continued to traverse backwards and forwards across the Atlantic until 1932, when she changed to cruising the calmer and less intimidating waters of the Mediterranean and throughout those of Northern Europe.

Having left Liverpool on Saturday, 8 October 1932 for a cruise around the beauty spots of Mediterranean, the 700 passengers on board the SS *Lancastria* had an unexpected yet exciting experience when the ship was called upon to assist the stricken Italian steamer, the *Scheldestad,* in the Bay of Biscay, where she rescued the twenty-one members of the ship's crew. Just prior to receiving the *Scheldestad*'s SOS, in the early hours of Monday 10 October, the *Lancastria* ran into a gale, but as soon as she received the distress call, she made all haste in the general direction of the damaged vessel.

The *Lancastria*'s skipper, Captain G.R. Dolphin received the message, 'Require immediate assistance'. In the meantime the *Lancastria* had received further news of the *Scheldestad* via a radio message which said, 'British steamer, *Burma* is at steamer *Scheldestad*, and we expect to sight her any minute.' This was excellent news for all concerned as at the time, the *Lancastria* was still some 50 miles away and cruising at a speed of about 14 knots. She quickly increased her speed, so beginning her involvement in the rescue of the *Scheldestad.*

The news of the emergency spread rapidly around the ship, with many passengers experiencing their first occasion of inclement weather as the *Lancastria* ploughed her way through the mountainous waves as she increased her speed to 19 knots. The distressed ship was sighted just after dawn, about half a mile away, and the passengers of the *Lancastria* who were up on deck were able to follow the events as they unfolded.

During the rescue another ship on the scene, an un-named oil tanker, circled the *Scheldstad* and poured about 40 tons of oil across the waters between herself and the stricken vessel. This had the effect of preventing the crest of the waves from breaking. It was a time-honoured solution to calm the sea between vessels in bad weather, although there may have been something of a risk of the oil catching fire. However, it must have been deemed a sensible thing to do, as the *Lancastria* did exactly the same.

When the *Lancastria* arrived on the scene she found that three other ships were standing by the *Scheldestad*, a vessel of some 4,800 tons, whose engine room had become flooded during the heavy weather. Disregarding the high seas, the *Lancastria* managed to lower a boat. The eleven crew members needed to row it were all volunteers who had been selected by the first officer, from a larger pool of volunteers. After a tremendous effort on the part of the lifeboat crew, they managed to pull alongside the *Scheldestad* and succeeded in rescuing the ship's crew. After everybody was safely on board via the ship's Jacob's ladder, the *Lancastria* sent the following brief radio message. 'Crew taken off. *Scheldestad* in sinking condition. Danger to navigation. *Lancastria* lifeboat also abandoned.' The crew of the *Lancastria's* lifeboat climbed back on board after the rescued sailors were safely aboard. The last man to leave the lifeboat was the first officer as the *Lancastria* was rolling some 25ft from side to side. He had just taken hold of the Jacob's ladder when the lifeboat buckled under his feet as it was repeatedly smacked against the side of the ship.

The Cunard company also received a message from the *Lancastria*, 'Rescue effected without casualties. Lifeboat cut adrift owing to heavy seas.' The company replied to the message with, 'Warmest congratulations on successful rescue work.'

The *Scheldestad* had belonged to the Scheldestroom Company of Ghent in Belgium but had been sold to an Italian firm and was on its way to Italy to be broken up, making the sinking somewhat ironic in the circumstances. Sadly for the holiday makers on board the *Lancastria,* they missed their stop in Lisbon, Portugal, as the ship had to make its way direct to Gibraltar to drop off the rescued crew. They evidently didn't mind too much as they had a collection for the crew members who had volunteered to take out the ship's lifeboat. The passengers also presented Captain Dolphin with an album that had been signed by all of them.

The *Lancastria* was requisitioned by the Admiralty in April 1940 and became a troopship with the prefix of HMT. She was first used during Operation Alphabet, which saw Allied troops being evacuated from Norway in May 1940, after which she underwent a small refit in Liverpool. She left there on 14 June 1940 under the command of Captain Rudolph Sharp, as part of Operation Aerial (the evacuation of Allied forces and civilians from ports in western France from 15 to 25 June 1940) and arrived off the French coast on 16 June, where she dropped anchor in the mouth of the Loire estuary, some 11 miles off St Nazaire.

By the afternoon of the following day an unknown number of men, women and children, civilian and military, had been embarked on to the *Lancastria*. The civilians included refugees, embassy staff and employees of the Fairey Aviation Company Limited, manufacturers of important British military aircraft. One thing that could be said for certain was that the number of people on board was in the thousands.

The exact number of those lost with the sinking of the *Lancastria* will never be known with any great degree of certainty. Many of those who died are still inside the hull of the ship, their bodies having never being recovered. Others would have been killed when the Luftwaffe bombs hit the ship. Bodies of British servicemen were washed up on the beaches around St Nazaire for weeks and months after the event. There were those who survived the initial sinking but died of their wounds in the days and weeks afterwards. Still more died in the sea as oil poured from the stricken ship and from the machine guns of the attacking aircraft.

The saddest thing of all about the sinking of the *Lancastria* is that there will be many men who died as a result of its loss, but whose family and friends will never know the true extent of how they were killed.

The man in charge of the *Lancastria*, Captain Rudolph Sharp, had, earlier in the day, been ordered by the Royal Navy to embark as many people as possible on to his ship, regardless to the official limitations as to how many passengers he was entitled to carry. Sharp was one of those who survived, but understandably, the loss of his ship and the estimated numbers who were lost with it, was an experience from which he never fully recovered, despite the fact that he had been powerless to prevent the attack by the Luftwaffe from taking place.

Almost unbelievably, on 12 September 1942, just over two years after the sinking of the *Lancastria*, HMT

Lanconia, which was also under the command of Captain Sharp, was also sunk, this time by two torpedoes fired by the German submarine, *U-156,* 130 miles north-east of Ascension Island in the South Atlantic Ocean. At the time of the attack, there were 1,800 Italian prisoners of war on board, most of whom were killed when the second torpedo struck the vessel. There were also 268 British soldiers and 160 Polish soldiers on board along with 80 civilians. It was quickly obvious to Captain Sharp that his ship was sinking and that there would be no saving it. He ordered that the wounded, women and children be placed in lifeboats ahead of all military personnel on board.

This time Captain Sharp did not survive. Whether by choice or otherwise, he was one of the estimated 1,658 individuals who were lost when the *Laconia* was sunk and in the immediate aftermath. This included 1,394 Italian prisoners of war of the 1,809 who had been on board.

The incident became infamous because not only did the German submarine, *U-156,* surface to pick up survivors, but called in several other German submarines to come and assist her. Despite clearly displaying Red Cross flags and Kapitanleutnant Werner Hartenstein having transmitted an open radio message that a rescue mission was under way, a US B-24 Liberator aircraft was ordered by senior American officer, Robert Charlwood Richardson III, who was unaware of Hartenstein's radio message, to attack the German submarines, which still had some of the survivors from the *Laconia* on their decks and in attached lifeboats that they were towing. The Germans had no choice but to dive and abandon the survivors they had previously rescued.

Despite Richardson being unaware of a rescue mission being under way when he ordered that attack, the pilot of the B-24 Liberator, could not possibly have missed the Red Cross flags on the German submarines, so why he carried out his attack is unclear.

Back to the *Lancastria*. On the day that she was sunk she was advised by the captain of the British destroyer, HMS *Havelock*, that she was free to depart and make her way back to England after the nearby troopship HMT *Oronsay* had been struck on her bridge by a German bomb just before 2pm. As the *Lancastria* did not have a destroyer escort to protect her from potential attack by German submarines, Captain Sharp, decided that he should wait for one to arrive.

Nearly four hours later, with the *Lancastria* still waiting for her destroyer escort, she was attacked by a number of Junkers Ju 88 aircraft from the Luftwaffe's bomber wing, Kampfgeschwader 30. The ship suffered four direct hits and sank within twenty minutes. Not content with knowing they had sunk the ship, the aircraft began strafing survivors floundering in the water. Leaking oil from the *Lancastria* gushing into the sea greatly hindered those survivors who were bobbing helplessly up and down in the water, left with nothing other than hope that they would be rescued before they were killed.

For years afterwards many families of those who lost their lives on the *Lancastria* did not know how their loved ones had died. All they knew was that they had been killed whilst serving with the British Expeditionary Force in France.

Despite Winston Churchill issuing a D-Notice to prevent news of the disaster reaching the public, an article about the tragedy appeared in the *New York Times* on 25 July 1940, which British newspapers took as the green light to report the incident in the pages of their publications.

The **Liverpool Evening Express** of the same day reported on the **New York Sun** newspaper's earlier article on the incident.

> *Boats and rafts were machine gunned by German planes which bombed and sank the Cunard White Star liner,* Lancastria *off Brest, according to a report in the* New York Sun *newspaper.*
>
> *The* Lancastria, *16,243 tons, was carrying 6,000 people when she was attacked, says the newspaper, and 500 were lost.*
>
> *During the evacuation from France, bombing planes made their attack as the embarkation was completed and scored three hits with aerial torpedoes, adds the* New York Sun. *One entered the funnel and exploded in the boiler-room. The liner sank in a few minutes.*
>
> *When the planes returned to machine gun boats and rafts a score of men were killed on one raft, according to eye witnesses who said it afforded an easy target from the air. If the machine gun fire aim had been as accurate as that of the bombs, they said, the losses would have been much greater.*
>
> *The* Lancastria *was lying with both bow-anchors down when she was attacked. She was struck fore and aft as well as in the funnel.*

Captain Sharp's life was saved by the ship's surgeon, Dr Shaw, says the newspaper.

The boats had been loaded quickly and Captain Sharp was the last man aboard. As the Lancastria *began to sink, he was struggling in the water, when Dr Shaw, who is a strong swimmer, dived from a boat and rescued him.*

Commander Sharp, Royal Naval Reserve, of the Lancastria, *resides in Grove Road, Wallasey.*

It is interesting to note that the number of fatalities mentioned in the article, is 500. Where or how that figure was arrived at was not clarified. The claim that Captain Sharp was the last man on board the *Lancastria* before she sank, is clearly incorrect.

An almost identical article appeared in the **Liverpool Echo** the same day, whilst the **Birmingham Mail** carried an extremely interesting piece about the *Lancastria's* demise on Saturday 27 July.

One who survived the sinking was Staff Quartermaster Sergeant P.H. Fairfax from Birmingham who had been serving with the Advanced Air Striking Force in France. So bad an ordeal was his experience, that he was discharged from the Army. He kept a diary of his war time experiences in France including an entry for the sinking of the *Lancastria.*

There was a terrific explosion, I rushed out on deck to learn that a bomb had dropped in the water alongside our ship. We heard all ships firing their guns and down came one plane.

The ship was now beginning to rock and everyone was trying to keep order. I then took a stroll to another part of the ship when away went the guns again and down came a dive plane and with one terrible bang he got us. She shook from head to stern and I knew it had gone home. I could hear the men below moaning and shouting.

The entry in Sergeant Fairfax's diary goes on to describe how the men on deck took to the water and as they were swimming around they had to protect themselves as best they could from the debris, rifles and other equipment which slithered down the sloping decks. Before he made his way off the deck and into the water, he helped some women into one of the lifeboats.

It was now impossible to climb the deck. I stood wondering when I would, as a non-swimmer, take to the water. The ship then went completely on its side and as it did so the lifeboat above crashed to the side of the ship but never released itself.

Fully clothed I took to the water with a cushion under my left arm and at the same time I grabbed a plank of wood which turned over as I put my right arm over it, so I let it go. The movement of the ship sent me right out to sea with the wreckage. I floated for some time until a raft with about ten men on it and around it, joined me. I felt below this and found a loop of rope. I put my right arm in this and with my cushion under my left arm I floated for some time, holding short conversations with the others and looking around.

During this time in the distance we saw a very
large raft with about 30 men on it, and heard the
old song, 'Roll out the barrel.'

Fairfax also described how, whilst bobbing about in the
water on the wooden rafts, he and his comrades were
attacked by German aircraft and strafed with machine-
gun fire, but thankfully none of them were injured. They
were on the wooden rafts for about four hours in total and
were picked up by a French merchant ship just before 9pm.

The Member of Parliament for Eye, in Suffolk, Mr E.L
Granville, of the Liberal Nationalist Party, was at a loss to
understand that why news of the bombing and sinking of
the *Lancastria,* and the story of the heroism of the British
troops on board, was not published in this country until
after it had appeared in the American Press. Mr Granville
obviously hadn't been taken into the confidence of
Winston Churchill. The more interesting point here was
that some of the men who had survived the sinking of the
Lancastria and had been instructed not to speak about
their experiences and what they knew, were more than
happy to talk openly about what they witnessed.

There was a large piece in the **Northern Whig and
Belfast Post** dated Friday 26 July. The article was headed
'How *Lancastria* Went Down – Women and Children
Machine Gunned'.

Nearly 2,500 are known to have been saved, and
more may be in enemy hands, from the 5,300
soldiers, airmen and civilian refugees aboard the
transport Lancastria, *which it was revealed last*
night, was sunk by enemy bombs on June 17 when

*about to weigh anchor at St Nazaire during the
evacuation of the British Expeditionary Force
from France.*

It is noticeable how the figures that were initially quoted
in the *New York Sun* were quite different from some of
the subsequent reports in British newspapers over the
following days. The article continued:

*Men, women and children, floundering in the
oil-blacked water, were subjected to murderous
machine-gun fire from the swooping 'planes'.
Tommies, packed so tight that they could not
move, jeered as the first bomb struck the ship.
Then they sang 'Roll out the Barrel' and as the
16,000-ton liner went down, 'There'll Always be
an England'.*

Two Church Army Sisters told of their experiences:

*We got into a lifeboat while men were sliding into
the sea by ropes, and others leapt overboard. The
German planes swept down and we saw the spurts
as their bullets struck the water where men were
swimming for their lives. Twenty-five men were
hanging like grim death to a piece of wood which
was too small to float, but none of them would
let go.*

*As our boat moved from the ship, soldiers watching
through a porthole saw that we were wearing our
lifebelts. They shouted, 'Give us a chance' and*

THE BIRTH OF A LEGEND 13

we flung the belts into the sea, and a number of soldiers jumped in after them. Then we threw our oars overboard. We saw RAF aeroplanes drop a number of life belts.

There were about one hundred women, children and soldiers in our lifeboat. Some boats sank as they were lowered, owing to the liner's list. When the first warship arrived, there was a great cheer and cries of 'The Navy's here'.

Other survivors spoke of how, when the *Lancastria* heeled over, men could be seen clambering on the ship's side in the belief that the stricken vessel would remain afloat, but within thirty minutes of being bombed, she sank beneath the waves, throwing all of those who had been on her side, into the water. A short while later, where the *Lancastria* had been moments earlier, the area was suddenly smothered in oil from the sinking ship.

Most of those who survived had spent more than an hour in the oily water trying not to swallow any of the oil whilst they waited to be picked up by a passing ship. When they arrived in England, many of them had lost their footwear and were walking about the quayside barefoot. How they had survived the cold waters for so long was a miracle. Many had either lost or removed their uniforms when they jumped into the water and only had blankets wrapped tightly around their bodies to keep themselves warm. They were too dazed and distressed to talk about their experiences, which they could have done freely at the time, as they wouldn't have been told not to until sometime later.

Besides the walking wounded and the mental anguish displayed on the faces of many of the survivors, there were a number of men who because of their injuries were brought out from the ships on stretchers.

An unnamed officer told reporters about the exemplary conduct of his men in extraordinary circumstances:

The men were simply magnificent. We were so tightly packed on board, that we could not move when the German aircraft flew overhead, so the men just jeered. When the bomb struck us, some were killed, but there was not the least sign of panic, and as the ship heeled over, those who were not thrown into the sea clambered on to her side and began to sing, but when they heard cries from men in the water, the singing stopped. When the ship went down it was a dreadful sight to see all those heads bobbing about in the water.

A member of the crew said: 'Beneath where I had been sitting I know there were at least 200 RAF men and they must have been lost. They just didn't have a chance. Their means of escape was cut off and I heard the terrible sound of their cries as I scrambled to safety.'

The cook said that the second bomb killed all of those in the ship's hospital, numbering about twelve, including the doctor. The Lancastria *gave a terrific lurch. I was flung into the sea, which can only be described as an almost solid mass of*

*men clinging together like flies and covered with
thick black oil.*

*The sights were frightful. Men clung to others
in the hope of survival. They bobbed about
everywhere. Some were horribly burnt by the
explosion. Others were hanging on to the debris.
It was every man for himself. All the time three
aeroplanes swooped and bombed the oily waters
and their machine gunners fired on the men
struggling for their lives.*

It is believed that the aircraft referred to were Italian and
one of those whose bombs made the direct hits on the
Lancastria is believed to have been shot down later by
another British vessel and the uninjured pilot was taken
prisoner. The Italians only entered the Second World War
on 10 June 1940.

The **Western Mail** dated Friday 26 July, was one
of the British newspapers which decided to report the
sinking of the *Lancastria*, despite the D-Notice that had
been placed on the incident at the insistence of Winston
Churchill.

Major Frank Golightly, a Durham County member of
the Salvation Army, said there was no panic:

*The boats were swung out and we helped to load
them with the women and children and some of
the wounded. Everything was done as quickly
as possible. I stayed as long as I could be of any
use and then slipped over the side of the ship. A
Frenchman in a cobble boat saw me and pulled
me in.*

An officer of the Royal Engineers was waiting on the quay at St Nazaire, to be taken out to the *Lancastria*. Luckily for him, he had not yet been transported out to the vessel, and so witnessed everything unfold in front of him from the quayside. He saw the bombs drop from the attacking aircraft and then watched helplessly as it first listed on to its side, then sank beneath the waves. He described what he did next:

> *I rushed to a nearby French tug and asked the crew to go out with me into the harbour to pick up survivors. An English Army doctor came with me. The men we picked up were coated with oil and were as black as coal miners. We made three trips and I reckon we saved at least 300 people, including some women. Other tugs were doing the same thing, so it is hoped that many hundreds were saved in all.*

A Welshman from Rhondda, Private W.R. Jones, who had survived the incident, was visiting his mother and stepfather, Mr and Mrs Cornelius Gronow, at their home in Brewery Street, Pontygwaith. He described how he saw and heard British soldiers and sailors, singing 'Roll out the Barrel' as the *Lancastria* sank, immediately prior to which they had been sitting on its side:

> *I was on a troopship six miles off the coast of south-western France, when German aeroplanes swooped down out of the sun and bombed the*

boat next to us. The enemy aeroplane, which was joined by two others, afterwards began bombing and made several direct hits, and the ship listed.

There was a scramble for the lifeboats but there was difficulty in getting them away. I dived into the water full of people. I was in the sea an hour and as my only garment, my shirt hampered me, I discarded it.

I could see the boat disappearing. Those still on it sang as it sank. One wounded man trapped in a porthole waved his hand in a cheering good-bye.

I was picked up by a trawler. When I landed in England my only covering was some sacking.

The point that strikes me in all of these reports is that not one of them makes any mention about how cold the water was, although many had discarded most of their clothes before jumping in.

It was reported in the *Newcastle Journal* on Saturday 27 July that two Darlington soldiers were survivors from the sinking of the *Lancastria*. They were Lance Corporal R. Fawcett of Danesmoor Crescent, Darlington, and Corporal Maurice Nixon, son of Mr and Mrs E. Nixon of Napier Street, Darlington.

The *Daily Record*, a Scottish newspaper, reported on Saturday 27 July how two men from Kilmarnock in Ayrshire, described their experiences of the sinking of the *Lancastria* in letters home to their families.

Sapper Sam Burnett of the Royal Engineers wrote that one bomb fell on the ship and that it almost immediately started to list to the starboard side:

We knew then that it was all up. What a scrabble there was for boats. Hundreds jumped into the water. A number of us got into a lifeboat, but it was jammed and could not be lowered so everyone got out except three of us. We arranged to stay on and as soon as the boat reached the water, we would cut the ropes.

By this time the ship was right over on its side and sinking fast, but we stuck to our boat and as soon as it reached the water we cut the ropes as arranged. But we only had the ropes cut when twenty or thirty men who were in the water, caught hold of the boat at one end and underneath she went after all our good work.

I had to strike out for anything I could get. After that Jerry came back and machine gunned us in the water. Then the oil tanks burst and the sea was just a mass of oil. After 2½ hours in the water I was picked up by a small French motorboat and taken back to St Nazaire.

The next night, Sapper Burnett and many others left France en route to England on board a British Royal Navy warship.

Another Kilmarnock man, Private Daniel Bolland, Royal Army Service Corps, wrote home to his parents with similar experiences of the sinking. He told of how, '*hundreds of the boys were standing on the ship's side as she was going under singing, "Roll out the Barrel", many of them marching off into the sea at the time.*'

The **Sunderland Daily Echo** dated Wednesday 31 July included a front page article which included the heading:

Sinking of the *Lancastria* – Why Information was Withheld

Mr Duff Cooper, Minister of Information, spoke in the House of Commons on Wednesday 31 July 1940, and gave the government's reasons for withholding the news of the bombing and sinking of the Lancastria, *said this ship was engaged in military operations, and it was evident from a German wireless announcement that the enemy were totally unaware of the identity of the ship sunk.*

It was contrary to the Government's general policy to announce the loss of individual merchant ships, but the number and total tonnage lost are given in weekly statements. The Lancastria's *tonnage was included in the statement issued on 2 July 1940.*

This policy was well known, and he could not therefore understand why on this occasion, bewilderment should have been caused in Liverpool and in shipping circles.

Mr E. Granville, the Liberal Member of Parliament for Eyre, declared that the story of the heroism connected with the Lancastria *was known on Merseyside two or three days after the sinking. It was afterwards given out on the German wireless and appeared in a New York paper. It was not until five weeks later that the story was referred to in a BBC news bulletin. Mr Granville said there was considerable anxiety in the public mind about this delay.*

Mr Duff Cooper replied that there were many stories of heroism connected with the Dunkirk evacuation, and this was one which he regretted did not get the full publicity it deserved.

Asked by Mr D.G. Logan, representing the Socialist Party of Scotland, why those most concerned were not informed earlier of the ship's loss, Mr Duff Cooper replied that relations of those lost were informed as soon as identity was established.

Mr A.V. Alexander, the First Lord of the Admiralty, said he could not agree to give information about Italian or German submarines that have been captured, sunk or damaged. Our silence prevented the enemy from discovering how these things happened and from gauging the efficiency of our anti-submarine methods. Such knowledge would be invaluable to the enemy.

Mr J.J. Davidson, the Socialist Member of Parliament for Glasgow, Maryhill, asked the somewhat humorous question: 'Is it true that British ships at sea call out, "Waiter" and Italian submarines come to the top?'

The question, which did not receive a reply, was greeted with noticeable laughter from all corners of the House.

The **Staffordshire Sentinel** dated Saturday 27 July, included an article concerning the sinking of the *Lancastria*. It included an account from Private J.B. Lewis, whose home was at 7 Jug Bank, Cobridge, Staffordshire.

Private Lewis, who was wounded when the *Lancastria* was bombed, said that he and his colleagues were on the beach at St Nazaire for three days and nights before they were embarked on to the *Lancastria*. During this time they were bombed and machine-gunned incessantly and the only food they were given was bully beef.

Private Lewis described his experience:

We heard the bombs falling and the anti-aircraft guns going all the time we were having dinner. Afterwards we went for a rest on our mattresses, but before long we heard that the German aircraft were coming over in formation. I went up on deck and was there when a bomb fell into the sea, 50 yards from the ship, followed by two more, even closer, which fell on either side of us.

Then we saw a dive-bomber swoop down. We rushed for cover, thinking he was going to machine gun us. There was a tremendous crash, and I was flung up against the rails. My limbs and trunk were completely numbed for a few minutes by the blast from the bomb, but at the time we did not realise that a bomb had hit the ship; we thought the bomber itself had crashed and we started to cheer. Then we found that a bomb had hit us and that the ship was in fact sinking.

As the ship began to list, I got over the rails and down to the rivets, and then a few minutes later, on to a screw-box, where I sat for a time. I shouted to a friend, 'Are you all right?' and he said that he was, but I think he was lost.

Near me a lot of men were on a raft, and they commenced to sing, 'Roll out the Barrel'. While they were on the raft a German bomber dived and swept it with machine-gun fire.

All the time, the planes were dropping flares on the surface of the water and bombing and machine-gunning went on all through the rescue work.

Although it could be argued that the *Lancastria* was a legitimate target, even though there were wounded soldiers on board, but it was not acting *per se* as a hospital ship, but what is totally unforgiveable is the conduct of the pilots of the attacking aircraft who, after dropping their bombs on the ship, fired on unarmed and defenceless men, women and children, who had taken to the water to save themselves. If that wasn't bad enough, they then dropped flares into the oil-sodden waters in an attempt to kill those they had missed with their machine guns, by burning them to death.

Private Lewis continued describing his personal experience of the sinking:

Gradually, the screw box, on which I was sitting, became submerged. I grabbed my belt and swam

off, and I later saw the ship go under. After
I had been in the water for nearly three and a
half hours, I was rescued, along with others by a
British warship. Nets were thrown over the side,
and we clung to these and were hauled aboard.

Along with other survivors, Private Lewis was taken to
England where he spent time recuperating in hospital
until he had fully recovered. Before the war he was in
the Army Reserve and was called up when the Germans
invaded Poland. He went to France early in the war
and had been there, except for a short period of leave,
until the evacuation at St Nazaire. A married man,
who in 1940 had an 11-year-old daughter, prior to the
war he had worked for the Shelton Iron, Steel and Coal
Company Ltd.

An article about Captain Sharp appeared in the
Aberdeen Press and Journal dated Friday 26 July. It
reported how he had been employed by the Cunard
company for some thirty years and had sailed in every
one of their ships, including as captain of the *Samaria,* the
Antonia and the *Lancastria.* He was a married man with
two children, the elder of whom was a lieutenant in the
Royal Navy. Having submitted his official report to the
Admiralty, Sharp would not at first discuss the matter with
members of the Press, but when approached at his home
in Wallasey, he was happy to engage with those present:

I was on the Bridge when the ship sank and I was
thrown into the water. I was supported for four
hours by my lifebelt. Then I saw one of my own
ship's lifeboats with an Irish Quartermaster and a

Scottish Quartermaster in charge. I hailed them and Murphy called to McLeod, 'Holy smoke, there's the Captain.'

There were several Frenchmen in the boat and with their help the two Quartermasters hauled me aboard. It was a tricky job, because I am pretty heavy and was as slippery as an eel owing to the oil on my clothing and lifebelt.

There is now reason to believe that other survivors may have made for the French coast.

One rating told of three or four men who had survived and were discovered floating on a makeshift wooden raft who were so dazed by their experience that they 'went crackers'. He said, 'We had to give them a smack to bring them to.'

The **Lancashire Evening Post** included an article on Friday 26 July, about one of the survivors, Private Arthur Howorth, of the Royal Army Service Corps, the son of Mr and Mrs Lord Howorth of 23 St Matthew's Street, Burnley, Lancashire. He was saved after swimming away from the stricken vessel until he reached the safety of a French fishing trawler, from which he was transferred to a Royal Naval destroyer. Private Howorth had attended Burnley Grammar School, where he was noted as being a keen sportsman, excelling at both rugby and tennis.

The **Birmingham Mail** of Friday 26 July included numerous articles about the sinking of the *Lancastria* which made for interesting reading. It mentioned how one of the ship's cooks saw a soldier rescue a young girl whose legs were broken; both were later rescued but sadly the girl died.

A Birmingham man who survived the sinking of the *Lancastria,* Corporal Fred Purchase of the Royal Army Service Corps, whose home was at 44 Upper Gough Street, Birmingham, was with two comrades, one from Darlington and the other from the Channel Islands. They had served together since the beginning of the war and had fallen back from Arras to the Loire after the collapse of the French Army and slept on the dockside at St Nazaire before embarking on the *Lancastria.*

Corporal Purchase spoke of epic British bravery:

> *The pluck shown by those fellows in that water made us proud to be called members of the British Expeditionary Force. There were hundreds of stories of individual bravery among the men swimming for their lives, those who could not swim but sat and sang on the side of the* Lancastria *before her final plunge, and among the others who quietly dropped in to the water not knowing whether they would come up again or not.*
>
> *My own officer dived into the sea with a baby girl of about three in his arms and I was glad to see that he had escaped, when I later saw the little girl and her mother on the troopship that rescued us. I remember an Air Force man who could not swim. He asked another man if he could swim, and then handed him his life belt saying, 'You may escape, I cannot swim.'*
>
> *When I was in the water two men floated past supporting another who could not swim. 'Are you all right?' they called out. 'Yes,' I told them. 'Then get hold of his legs.'*

It was this type of spirit and bravery which stood out for Corporal Purchase in his time as a soldier since he was called up as a supplementary reservist from the parcels section of the Birmingham General Post Office. After he finally arrived back in England, he was given nine days leave before he had to report back to his unit. He said:

At St Nazaire, German planes, probably on reconnaissance, came over during the Sunday night. At ten o'clock the following morning we got on board the Lancastria. *At mid-day a German raider appeared but his bombs missed our boat. Just after the ship had completed loading, about four o'clock in the afternoon, I and my pals were going down to the mess room when warning bells sounded and the raid began.*

I was on deck and orders were shouted to take cover in case of machine gunning. I actually got down to the mess room when an aerial torpedo, which is larger than a bomb with vanes on it, came through. We were blown off our feet by the blast and dust and smoke were everywhere. Someone turned to me and said, 'That's us.' Immediately the Lancastria *started to list. I heard a shout, 'Make way for the women and children.'*

That was the first I knew of the presence of women and children on the ship. A passage was made for them and they were got away. Then we were told 'Every man for himself.' But there was no panic. Some were able to march up on deck. We three pals separated and did not meet again until after we were rescued. I meandered along the passageways to the deck. By that time the Lancastria *was going down by the bows. The boats that could be got away were launched. She was going down, down so rapidly you could hardly keep your feet. Still there was no panic and some men were asking each other what they were going to do next. Others were calmly taking off their clothes. Everything that could float had been hurled overboard. The list was developing towards the final capsizing.*

I went down the side by a wire rope and started to swim away from her. My hands were torn by the rope and injured during the operation. I was able to get hold of a piece of wood in the water.

My last impressions of the Lancastria *were of crowds of men on the side singing 'Roll out the Barrel' and other popular tunes. They knew it was impossible for them to get away. Then their last song was 'There'll always be an England'. She turned over and went down bows first. It was all over in about 20 minutes.*

The water was thick with oil and some men were choked by it. Others were scalded by the steam. Then the Nazi planes came over us and machine gunned the men, women and children in the water. They bombed us in the water.

How we cheered, men in the water, men, women and children in boats and on rafts, when a warship brought down the pilot and plane that had sunk this ship.

For four hours I was in the water, swimming and hanging on to my piece of wood. Eventually a lifeboat picked me up and I was transferred to a French tug. When I got on to the troopship that finally brought me to a West Country port, I found one of my pals and the other turned up later. I arrived at the troopship naked, covered in grease and with my hands injured.

Those other soldiers on that vessel were magnificent. They threw us packets of cigarettes, they even tipped out their kit bags and gave us their spare clothes. I got a pair of old trousers, an old shirt, socks and an old tunic. A captain, an elderly man in the Auxiliary Military Pioneer Corps, was going round off his own bat dressing our wounds.

British people can be magnificent. Besides the clothes, we were fed, supplied with cigarettes, money and had everything given to us we could want. Those people deserve our thanks. It must have cost them something. We never expected kindness, but I am afraid you could not print the name we used for those Nazis.

Friday 26 July saw the **Birmingham Evening Despatch** include an article concerning the sinking of the *Lancastria*. One of the thirty or forty men from Birmingham who had been on board the *Lancastria* when she was attacked was Private John Ames of the Pioneer Corps. He was 38 years of age and a married man with five children, whose home was at 204 Queens Road, South Yardley, Birmingham.

After jumping into the water where he spent some four hours, he was rescued by a French fishing boat from the danger of the withering machine-gun fire of the attacking enemy aircraft. But fearing being captured by the Germans and becoming a PoW for the duration of the war, he nearly jumped overboard when he realised that his rescuers were taking him back to France. After eventually making it back to 'Blighty', he got to spend some time with his wife and children before having to report back to his unit on Friday 26 July.

The following is the story of his *Lancastria* experience told to a reporter from the ***Birmingham Evening Despatch***:

> *The* Lancastria *was at anchor at St Nazaire, and we reached her in a small boat. It took us an hour to reach her. She was packed with soldiers, mostly Pioneers like myself with dozens of women and children refugees.*
>
> *Among the Pioneers, there were to my knowledge some 30 or 40 Birmingham men. Enemy planes made several attempts to get us, and when the final salvo got us, just before four o'clock in the afternoon the ship went right over. She was down in about 30 minutes.*
>
> *I saw one lifeboat get away. In it was a Belgium woman with two young children. While the* Lancastria *was still above water, we clung to the sides. When she went down, we tried to reach floating pieces of timber, but there was so much*

oil about that we kept slipping off. Meanwhile the planes above were dropping bombs all around us. For four hours we were like that, swimming from one piece of timber to another, through patches of oil. Finally, we were picked up by a French fishing smack. But when they began taking us back towards the coast of France, I didn't know what to do. I was beginning to wonder whether I wouldn't prefer risking the bullets and water out there rather than be a prisoner, that was my biggest fear.

However, after a night in hospital, a British ship brought us back to dear old 'Blighty'. As we set out, a plane came over and dropped a bomb uncomfortably near. But it was the last bomb he'll drop. A gun from a warship brought him down. We got back to England and this afternoon I report for duty again.

It was subsequently pointed out that a number of the survivors were admitted to hospital suffering with scalds, caused by the explosion of the boilers. This had probably given rise to the story that the oil on the water was ignited by incendiary bombs.

On Saturday 27 July an article appeared in the **Shields Daily News**, concerning a local man, Private Thomas McDonald whose home was at 18 Laburnum Avenue, Ridges Estate, North Shields and who had survived the sinking. A 38-year-old married man with five children, he had been called up at the beginning of the war, initially as a Territorial. Despite his small stature he was one of the trickiest centre forwards in the North Eastern League and was well known in Tyneside footballing circles. He played for the old Preston Colliery team, with whom he was a prolific goal scorer. Before commencing his military service, he was a member of the Bishopsgate House Social Centre and had appeared in several of their plays.

On Monday, 29 July 1940, the *Liverpool Evening Express* reported how Robert Henry King, a 24-year-old ship's steward who lived with his parents, Mr and Mrs Edward King, at High Park Street, Toxteth, Liverpool, had survived. Robert King jumped into the sea with the ship's captain at the last minute. He was picked up by another vessel after having been in the water for more than two hours. By the time the article appeared in the newspaper he had already been allocated to another Cunard ship.

There were many similar articles about the sinking of the *Lancastria* which appeared in the *Birmingham Daily Gazette*. The *Dundee Evening Telegraph*, the *Liverpool Evening Express,* the *Hartlepool Northern Daily Star*, the *Birmingham Evening Despatch*, the *Nottingham Evening Post*, the *Yorkshire Post & Leeds Intelligencer*, the *Dundee Courier*, the *Hull Daily Mail,* the *Newcastle Journal*, the *Daily Mirror*, the *Daily Herald*, the *Lancashire Evening Post*, *The Scotsman*, which reported, '*nearly 2,500 are known to have been saved from a total of 5,300 aboard, and more may be in enemy hands*', the *Western Morning Star*, the *Western Daily Press*, the *Manchester Evening News*, the *Daily Record*, the *Falkirk Herald*, the *Birmingham Daily Post*, the *Birmingham Mail*, the *Portsmouth Evening News*, the *Newcastle Evening Chronicle*, the *Express and Echo* and the *Aberdeen Weekly Journal*, to name but a few.

CHAPTER 2

Operation Cycle

Squeezed in between Operation Dynamo and Operation Aerial was Operation Cycle, the evacuation of Allied troops from the port of Le Havre which took place between 10 and 13 June 1940.

On 5 June 1940, in the final couple of weeks of the Battle of France, German forces began their final offensive. Part of the 9th Army Corps of the French Tenth Army included the British 51st (Highland) Division under the command of Major General Victor Fortune, part of the British Expeditionary Force. German tanks entered Rouen on 9 June 1940 and in doing so they cut off the 9th Army Corps from the French 10th Army Corps. The British and French commanders quickly realised that they ran the risk of being encircled by the Germans if they did not act quickly.

The decision was made to make for the French port of Le Havre, even though Major General Fortune had been given orders by the French General Robert Altmayer, commander of the French 10th Army Corps, and the War Office in London, to make his way to the River Seine, through an area that he knew was occupied by a number of German divisions. To ensure that they could make their way speedily and safely to Le Havre, Arkforce, an *ad hoc* formation of the British Expeditionary Force, was given the task of forming a defensive line that stretched for a distance of about 19 miles, to the east of Le Havre. Once in position, they would allow the 51st (Highland) Division, along with the rest of 9th Army Corps to retreat to Le Havre. Once that had been achieved, Arkforce then had the job of providing a defensive line, closer to the port area, to enable the larger, main body of men to be safely evacuated.

That was the plan and plans always look good when they are written down on paper or across a map, but that doesn't always mean they are going to work out as expected. This was one of those occasions. The roads to Le Havre were, as might be expected in the circumstances, congested by human traffic and abandoned vehicles, which meant that anticipated timings were hard to keep to. What didn't help matters was that elements of the German 7th Panzer Division had driven between Arkforce and the 9th Army Corps, although most of Arkforce had already passed through before their arrival. With this route now not viable for the main body of 9th Corps to make good their escape, they changed direction and headed towards St Valery-en-Caux in Normandy.

Between 10 and 11 June 3,321 British and French troops were rescued from St Valery by the Royal Navy but not everybody was so fortunate. On 12 June, more than 6,000 soldiers from the 51st (Highland) Division were captured when, surrounded and with no chance of evacuation by the Royal Navy, Major General Victor Fortune was forced to surrender to General Erwin Rommel.

Despite the problems caused by the intervention of the German 7th Panzer division, 11,000 British troops of Arkforce along with other British units, made it through to Le Havre and were evacuated by a combination of vessels of the Royal Navy, Canadian Royal Navy and Dutch coasters known as *schuyts*, which were flat bottomed barges used for carrying cargo rather than people. They had been sent over by the Commander-in-Chief Portsmouth, Admiral William James. The flotilla of boats, which included six British destroyers and two Canadian destroyers, were led by HMS *Codrington.*

CHAPTER 3

Operation Aerial

Operation Dynamo, or as it is more commonly referred to, the Dunkirk evacuations, is a widely known piece of military history of the Second World War which resulted in more than 300,000 British and Belgian troops, mainly infantry personnel, being evacuated from the beaches of Dunkirk. It was a defining moment of the war, because if all those men had been captured or killed that would have been the war over at that time and Britain would have had to either surrender to Germany or negotiate a peace deal.

What is not so widely known is Operation Aerial which took place between 15 and 25 June 1940 and entailed the evacuation of Allied military and civilian personnel following the collapse of the Battle of France with forces of Nazi Germany.

British and Allied ships that had been sent across the English Channel from Plymouth, Poole, Weymouth, Portsmouth and Southampton to collect stranded British military and civilian personnel, were covered in their rescue mission by five fighter squadrons of the Royal Air Force (RAF) from French bases and assisted by further aircraft based in England, to lift British, Polish and Czech troops, civilians and equipment from a number of Atlantic ports, particularly from St Nazaire and Nantes, but also Cherbourg, St Malo, Brest, La Pallice, Le Verdon, Bordeaux, Bayonne and Saint-Jean-de-Luz.

The Luftwaffe began attacking evacuation ships and on 17 June managed to evade RAF fighter patrols and sink the Cunard liner and wartime requisitioned troopship, HMT *Lancastria* in the Loire estuary. The ship sank quickly and whilst efforts were underway to rescue survivors, other vessels in the immediate vicinity, were also under attack. The rescue operation saved approximately 2,500 evacuees and members of the crew. Despite no available official numbers of those who perished in the attack, the loss of the *Lancastria* is still held up as being the maritime disaster with the greatest loss of life in a British ship.

As well as troops and civilian personnel, part of the operation had also allowed for the embarkation of military equipment, but because even routine intelligence wasn't readily available, many pieces of equipment were either destroyed or left behind, because of concerns about how far away the advancing German forces were. The final evacuations from ports on the west coast of France of either men or equipment had to be completed by 25 June 1940, as the Armistice that had been signed by France and Germany came into force as from 26 June although departures from ports along the French Mediterranean coastline continued until 14 August 1940.

Subsequent to the evacuations from the beaches at Dunkirk as part of Operation Dynamo there was Operation Cycle which took place between 10 and 13 June 1940, from Le Havre, which was followed by Operation Aerial. As a result of the latter two operations, a further

191,870 Allied troops were rescued from German occupied France, bringing the total number of military and civilian personnel brought safely back to the south coast of England to 558,032.

Operation Aerial was again led by Admiral William James, the Commander-in-Chief at the Portsmouth naval base. James simply did not have a sufficient number of vessels to run convoys, so instead he organised a number of troopships, store ships, coasters, motor vehicle vessels and other types of ships to leave from ports along the south coast of England, while the Royal Navy warships that were available, patrolled the main shipping routes that the evacuation ships followed. Royal Engineer demolition parties sailed in the ships, just in case some equipment had to be left behind, but it was hoped that all supplies and equipment could be embarked as well as troops. None of it could be allowed to fall into the hands of the enemy.

Part of the problem during Operation Aerial was the air support that was available to cover the evacuations from St Nazaire – or rather the lack of it. After German forces started to gain the upper hand in the Battle of France on 11 June 1940, the Air Ministry in London warned Air Vice-Marshal Arthur Barratt, who was in command of the British Air Forces in France, that the Germans would soon be upon them and to make ready to leave France at very short notice. Taking note of this information, Barratt moved many of his squadrons to the comparative safety of French bases in the west, but these bases were already heavily congested with French aircraft. If the Luftwaffe had carried out just one air raid on many of these airfields, they would have potentially taken out a disproportionate number of Allied aircraft. Possibly with this in mind, Barratt took the decision to send all of his light bombers back to England, an event which took place on 15 June 1940, leaving just five fighter squadrons in France to cover the evacuations.

The ports of Nantes and St Nazaire, which were the two central ports for the evacuations under Operation Aerial, had air cover provided by Nos. 1, 73 and 242 Squadrons, but in total they had seven ports for which they had to provide cover, which made it a potentially precarious situation for those on the ground. Aircraft from bases in the west of England were used to protect the returning vessels full of British troops and civilian employees.

Evacuations during Operation Aerial also took place from Cherbourg, Saint-Malo and Brest. During the operation a remarkable scenario took place, which on the surface sounds absolutely ridiculous. The Chief of the Imperial General Staff, Alan Brooke, was informed on 15 June 1940, that 'for political reasons' the two brigades of the 52nd Division could not be evacuated at that time, but he was given no an explanation. After some high-level phone conversations had taken place with those in London, the earlier decision was overturned in part; gunners from the artillery units could be embarked, but not infantry. Between 15 and 17 June most of the 52nd Lowland Division and remnants of the 1st Armoured Division were evacuated from Cherbourg and by the end of the day on 17 June the improvised units of the Beaumon Division and the Norman Forces defending Rouen had all been evacuated. By the end of the evacuations a total of 30,630 men, mostly British, had been rescued from Cherbourg and taken across the English Channel to Portsmouth. St Malo saw a successful evacuation take place with a total of 21,474 men rescued from there between 17 and 18 June, most of them coming from the 1st Canadian Division. The RAF did such a good job of protecting the evacuations at St Malo that not one ship was damaged and not one single soldier was wounded or killed.

The Belgian Countess de Pret arrived in London after escaping from St Malo, in a 10-metre yacht. She told the Press:

> *After all the scenes of panic in France, it was wonderful to see the calmness with which the British officers and soldiers carried out their duties at St Malo.*
>
> *Although the Germans were within a few miles of the place, the British made a thorough job of the demolition of St Malo harbour. They blew up everything, and the harbour will be out of use for at least two years. We also learned that the British had made Cherbourg useless as a port and had destroyed the harbour works there.*

With all of the evacuations, the strategy of not leaving anything behind that could be used by the enemy was paramount. This meant that any such plans the enemy might have had of utilising the same harbours and ports as Britain and her Allies, was gone, unless a lot of time, energy and manpower was spent repairing them. In fact, British naval forces in co-operation with the local French authorities, had completely demolished the harbour at St Malo. They destroyed millions of tons of petrol rather than let it fall into the hands of the enemy. The nearby aerodrome at St Malo was left in ruins as well.

Mr Le Marquand, a resident of St Malo, and the owner of a yacht, *Klang ll*, was one of those who saw the harbour at St Malo being destroyed and described his experiences when he arrived in England from Jersey:

> *After the troops had been evacuated, all of the locks were cleared of shipping, before the British naval officer in charge of the demolition party began his work at 2pm and finished at 3.25pm. Although the Germans were fast approaching St Malo, the rating worked coolly and systematically, as if carrying out a routine job.*
>
> *The officer in charge, alone took any of the risks. At one place only three of the charges exploded, although four of them had been laid. Some of the men wanted to go into the danger zone to find out what had happened. The officer refused to allow them to break cover. A few seconds later there was a deafening explosion and portions of the lock gates were hurled into the air. The officer still took no cover, standing alone while debris fell all around him. Sole casualty was one rating whose hand was injured by a splinter.*

British military vehicles including lorries and cars were all made unusable and then pushed into deep water. When Mr Le Marquand finally left St Malo, the harbour was a mass of flames and thick black smoke. Twelve hours later both could still be clearly seen from Jersey.

In fact, the last ship to leave from St Malo was a 30ft long yawl, the *Leonoite* owned by Mr W.P. Williams and his two companions, Mr J.W. Mabey, who was a butcher, and an unnamed Scottish traveller. Their job was to take off the Royal Navy demolition team who set off the charges. They had arrived off St Malo at dawn on 17 June, along with a host of other small boats, all of which were manned by civilians. On arrival they reported to the British naval commander and were told that a naval party were going to blow up the lock gates of the harbour, along with other demolition work around the harbour. It would be their job 'to stand by and take the party off when they had finished their task'.

Mr Williams and his two friends were asked by the naval commander to give him their word of honour that they would wait for the party to finish their work, as they would be the only means the men had of making good their escape. All three men gave their word. As the naval party finished laying all of their charges, it was reported that the Germans had arrived on the outskirts of the town. The last member of the naval party jumped on board the *Leonoite*, Mr Williams pushed off from the dock, and off they went into the unknown elements of the English Channel.

But their adventures were not quite over. The vessel ran into rain and heavy seas as dusk fell. The boat's engine failed after a huge wave descended upon them, which left it drifting aimlessly throughout the night. They were eventually taken in tow by a Belgian boat and made it safely to Jersey before later travelling home to Blighty.

CHAPTER 4

Secret Session Speeches

During the Second World War, the Prime Minister, Mr Winston Churchill, made a total of five speeches in secret session to the House of Commons. These were of such a sensitive nature and major importance that it was deemed at the time that the content of them could be useful to the enemy.

What might appear somewhat staggering by today's standards, is that none of these speeches were ever recorded for either official or historical purposes. However, fortunately for future generations, what Churchill had to say was of such significance that before delivering four of the speeches, he prepared full texts of what he was about to say. To avoid any accidental breaches of security and to ensure accuracy of the content, each of the speeches was checked by interested ministers before they were delivered by Churchill.

The notes and actual words of the speeches were kept by him when his time as Prime Minister came to an end. When the government which succeeded his ministry lifted the ban on revealing what had actually been said at each of these secret sessions Mr Charles Eade, who first put the notes of these secret sessions to print, was provided with the content of them and the authority to publish them by Churchill himself. There is, of course, now no way of proving today that the written content of what has been recorded, are the actual words that Churchill used in his secret session speeches, as he could have ad-libbed, missed words out or added bits, but they are as accurate as they can possibly be.

The five speeches were as follows:

The Fall of France – 20 June 1940
Parliament in the Air Raids – 17 September 1940
The Battle of the Atlantic – 25 June 1941
The Fall of Singapore – 23 April 1942
Admiral Darlan and the – 10 December 1942
    North Atlantic Landings

As can be seen, such speeches were a rarity throughout the years of the Second World War. The one of interest to this book is that which Churchill made on 20 June 1940, just three days after the sinking of the SS *Lancastria*. Sadly, out of the five Secret Session speeches made by Winston Churchill, during the Second World War, the only one where a copy of his speech has not survived, is the one he made concerning the Fall of France. Another point worth highlighting is that at the time of this particular Secret Session, Operation Aerial was taking place. It ran from 15 to 25 June 1940, with the sinking of the *Lancastria* taking place on 17 June, just three days before the Secret Session in the House of Commons. It surely would have been more productive, and certainly would have made more sense, to wait until Operation Aerial had concluded, so that Churchill could have provided the House with a full and comprehensive report of all aspects of the operation, good, bad or indifferent, rather than call for a Secret Session whilst it was still going ahead – that is of course unless a major and tragic event hadn't taken place.

Despite not having a copy of the actual speech made by Churchill at the Secret Session held on 20 June 1940, as it was the only one that he did not write down the full text of what he intended to say, we do have the notes made about that speech by Charles Eade that were given to him by Churchill.

> *On 18 June 1940, the Prime Minister made a full statement to the House of Commons about the situation created by the impending collapse of French resistance. He concluded with the words: 'Let us therefore brace ourselves to our duties, and so bear ourselves that, if the British Empire and its Commonwealth last for a thousand years, men will still say, "This was their finest hour."'*
>
> *The House went into secret session on June 20, when the French Government, headed by Marshal Pétain, had actually sought Armistice terms from Germany and Italy. When the Prime Minister rose in the House that evening to wind up the debate, he held nine pages of type written additions and alterations as the discussion proceeded. There is no full record of the speech he delivered. The other Secret Session speeches printed here were dictated beforehand and every argument and phrase carefully considered and checked. As this debating speech lasted more than an hour, and as the occasion was tragic and*

critical in the extreme, the following nine pages, with photographed reproductions of the notes he used, are of interest.

They show that he told the house he considered a Secret Session should be a normal part of its procedure and was necessarily associated with a crisis. He warned his listeners that it would be folly to underrate the gravity of the impending German attack but felt that, so far as the air raids were concerned, the people of Britain would get used to them. The enemy, he added, were not using their bombers very cleverly and our own bombing was far more effective.

Mr Churchill then discussed the Allies' military errors and failures on the continent and the melancholy position of the new French Government. He expressed his confidence in the strength of Britain's resisting power and added that if Hitler failed to invade or destroy Britain, he had lost the war. 'If we get through the next three months,' he wrote in his notes, 'we get through the next three years!'

He spoke of America's attitude to the war and emphasised that nothing would stir them so much as the news of fighting in England. He added: 'The heroic struggle of Britain is the best chance of bringing them in.'

Mr Churchill concluded by speaking of the formation of the new Government headed by himself and said he had a right to depend on

loyalty to his administration and to feel that we
had only one enemy to face – 'The foul foe who
threatens our freedom and our life, and bars the
upward march of man.'

I believe that it is inconceivable that Churchill would not have mentioned at a Secret Session in the House of Commons, details about Operation Aerial and the tragic loss of the *Lancastria* and all of those who were on board. There was also the success of the evacuations from Dunkirk. One way or another something about this just isn't right. Either Churchill did type a text of his speech, but simply didn't hand it over to Charles Eade, or Eade himself has been very selective about what he subsequently released in relation to what he is claiming Churchill actually said.

CHAPTER 5

The Sinking of the HMT *Lancastria*

Churchill was the person who decided that news of the sinking of the *Lancastria* should not be made public, because as he put it, the public had received enough bad news already and to give them even more would not be good for morale. He did this in the form of a D-Notice.

The D-Notice system had been in place since 1912 when the Admiralty and the War Office decided that they needed a way in which the government of the day could prevent information which might be of use to an enemy, or future enemy, from being published in the Press. On 13 August 1912, representatives from the Press Association, the War Office, along with the Secretary of the Admiralty, met to deal with the matter. An agreement was reached that an organisation would be set up that would include Press representatives, who were given assurances that only matters that really did affect the national interest and security of the nation, could even be considered for the Press not to print stories about, if the government requested them not to do so.

The members of the committee who would decide on such matters consisted of a representative from the War Office of the rank of at least an Assistant Secretary, along with a representative of the Press Association. Both individuals were appointed as joint Secretaries. It was agreed that if the Admiralty or the War Office had information of a military nature that they did not want published in the newspapers, the War Office would contact the Press Association representative and a meeting of the committee would be convened. Once the relevant information had been discussed, and an agreement of not to print had been reached, the Press Association representative would send a copy of the agreed D-Notice by hand to the editors of all London publications and to provincial editors in the form of telegrams which would be handed to them personally by the local postmaster.

It was in the early part of the war that D-Notices were replaced with press censorship, which came under the Ministry of Information. D-Notices were not always adhered to, intentionally or otherwise. In the House of Commons on Wednesday, 7 August 1940, the Liberal Nationalist Member of Parliament for the constituency of Eye, Mr Granville, asked why the loss of the *Lancastria,* while being used as a troopship to evacuate troops from France, was classified in the total tonnage of merchantmen lost; why no official account of the story of heroism, ranking with the gallantry of the Dunkirk evacuation was made by the Minister of Information, and if he would see that an official statement was made to alleviate the anxiety of dependants and relatives.

Mr Duff Cooper said the *Lancastria* was so classified because she was not one of HM Ships. She was only defensively armed, had no naval ratings or officers on board and she was not flying the White Ensign. The facts of the sinking so far as they were known had been published in this country and a full account was issued to the Press at the Ministry of information on 26 July 1940. As all the known facts had been stated, he feared that nothing further could now be done to alleviate anxiety.

Mr Granville then asked Mr Duff Cooper if he was aware that there were relatives and dependants still without news? Is there nothing further to be done? Mr Duff Cooper replied that it was not now possible to ascertain exactly who was on board the *Lancastria* when she was sunk.

Mr Duff Cooper was not correct when he said that the *Lancastria* was not one of HM ships as an explanation as to why her tonnage was included in the figures quoted and counted under merchant shipping. At the time of her sinking the *Lancastria* had the prefix of HMT, His Majesty's Troopship, so she definitely was a HM vessel.

On Saturday, 14 June 1941, the **Hastings and St Leonards Observer** printed a piece under their heading '*On Active Service*'. It read:

> *Captain Harold Burleigh, Royal Engineers, previously reported missing, now reported killed in action at sea in June 1940, as the result of the sinking of SS* Lancastria. *Beloved husband of Marion Burleigh of Stonelynk, Fairlight.*

Captain 107035 Harold Burleigh has no known grave but his name is commemorated on the Dunkirk Memorial, in the Nord region of France.

On Tuesday 17 June 1941, on the first anniversary of the sinking of the *Lancastria*, a remembrance notice was placed in the **Liverpool Echo**:

Price – Loving remembrance of our only son and brother, Aircraftsman Thomas Price, missing, SS Lancastria. *Lost a while but ever remembered. Mother and Dad, Peggy and Horace, Ethel and Frank, Marion and Jim, Nellie, Vera and Beryl, 4 Linwood Road, Birkenhead.*

Thomas was 20 years of age and a 2nd Class Aircraftsman in the RAF, when he was killed in action on 17 June 1940 whilst on board SS *Lancastria.* His body was not recovered but his name is commemorated on a memorial which is situated at the Pornic War Cemetery in the Loire-Atlantique region of France.

On Tuesday, 8 July 1941, the **Sunderland Daily Echo and Shipping Gazette**, published two 'in loving memory' notices in the Roll of Honour section. There were two notices for Frederick Jackson, who was 47 years of age, and had lived at 9 Ann Street, Hendon. The first was from his widow Pamela and their son James. The other was from his mother, brothers and sister. Both notices mentioned that he had initially been reported as missing in action, but that it had now been confirmed that he was killed in action on 17 June 1940 whilst on board the SS *Lancastria.*

There were a further two notices for Sydney Walton, who was killed in action at sea aboard the SS *Lancastria* on 17 June 1940, and who lived at 139 Chester Road. He was '*lovingly remembered by his wife Nora, and their daughter and sons'*. There was a separate notice from Sydney's sister in law, Jenny.

On Friday 18 July 1941, the **Dover Express** carried an article concerning Victor William Leighton, who was 37 years of age and served with the Pioneer Corps. He was killed on active service on 17 June 1940, by enemy action whilst at sea on board the SS *Lancastria*. Before the war Victor and his wife Beatrice, lived at 35 York Road, Dover, Kent. The Commonwealth War Graves Commission website shows Private 1300192 William Leighton, not Victor William. He was serving with the 53rd Company, Auxiliary Military Pioneer Corps. He has no known grave and his name is commemorated on the Dunkirk Memorial.

Saturday, 30 August 1941, saw an article in the **Surrey Advertiser** concerning Lance Corporal John Matthew Wild 6083113, who was 33 years of age and serving with the 1st Battalion, East Surrey Regiment. He was a married man having wed his wife, Mary, in January 1940. Their home was at 100 Station Road, Shalford, where Mary received notification that he was presumed to have been killed at sea whilst on board the SS *Lancastria* in June 1940.

Lance Corporal Wild was the eldest son of Mr and Mrs John Wild, of 7 Hurst Hill Cottages, Bramley. He had served with the East Surrey Regiment and was in India with them before being placed on the Army Reserve. He was recalled to the colours shortly after the outbreak of war and was sent out to France almost immediately.

On Friday, 12 June 1942, in the **Sevenoaks Chronicle and Kentish Advertiser** under the 'In Memoriam' heading, were two notices for Harry Derwin. The first was from his devoted wife Gladys:

> *In treasured memory of my dearly loved husband LAC Harry Derwin, RAF, who lost his life, SS* Lancastria, *June 17, 1940. 'In memory's garden I am with you every day.'*

The second was from his parents, which read:

> *In ever loving memory of our darling son, husband and brother, Harry, who lost his life on the 'Lancastria' June 17, 1940. Mum, Dad, Gladys, Kitty, Diana and Hamilton.*

Harry's parents also placed a similar In Memoriam notice in the same newspaper on Friday, 16 June 1944.

CHAPTER 6

Jesse 'Mickey' Fenton's Story

Whilst researching this book I made contact with Jo Fenton, having heard about her father's connection with the *Lancastria* disaster. She agreed that I could use her father's story in this book. Jo sent me her late father's war time story including his personnel account of the sinking of the *Lancastria*. His name was Jesse Fenton, although he was known to his friends and Army colleagues as 'Mickey'.

After he had been rescued from the aftermath of the sinking of the *Lancastria*, off St Nazaire, he was sent back home to England, and on arrival he initially found himself being sent to recover from his ordeal at the naval barracks just west of the city of Plymouth known as HMS *Drake*.

Read Jesse's story here in his own words and discover what a remarkable man he was:

> *After leaving HMS Drake and with instructions to keep quiet about the recent disaster, we were on our way again. Of course, in reality, we felt compelled to tell anyone who was willing to listen to a detailed account of the near death experience we had suffered and the actual number of lives that*

were lost. On the way people cheered as we went past on the train, as though we had won the war! Unlike France, where it felt proud to be a member of the British army, this felt unjust; we had just lost the war. They were honouring fraudsters. We had been running away from the enemy for the past few weeks, we were failures.

We stopped at Leeds for about four days. Whenever we went out of the flats we were continuously being stopped and reprimanded for not wearing hats. Before leaving the naval station, at Devenport we were only issued with battle dress, a towel, shoes, socks, one set of underwear and a piece of soap. By the third night we were extremely frustrated and felt harassed by the unjust reproach we were receiving. A sergeant was standing just outside the flats. He was from the military police known as the Red Caps. We strutted over to him. One of us spoke in a pleading, although demanding voice, 'Look sergeant, we've just come back from France. We've got no hats or anything. Are you going to object to us walking about without hats on?'

Normally the Red Caps are unreasonable and not very sympathetic, so we were pleasantly surprised when he answered without any hesitation, 'No, we know all about you.'

I cannot repeat what he told us to say to anyone else who stopped us. Well not without the expletives! After that we ignored anyone who dared to reprimand us.

For a while we were like lost sheep. There remained the sixteen of us from the Sherwood Foresters and we were herded to Skegness. The 2nd Battalion was stationed here and although we were supposed to join them, for some inexplicable reason they did not want us. Another train ride took us to Derby and back to Normanton Barracks where I had trained before going to France.

Of course, my family were delighted to see me but knew nothing about the Lancastria disaster. Contrary to instructions I continued to tell people about it. My beloved father believed me but due to a cynical landlord from the pub across the road, others in Radford thought I was telling elaborate stories. The publican actually said to my dad, 'You want to take no notice, Tommy, they make these things up when they come back.' This was a hurtful diminishing remark and I felt gratefully smug when a fortnight later the story, along with pictures, were in the papers. Although the tragedy of the disaster was to be lost from the people of Great Britain, hidden by the war, even though the loss of lives overshadowed many atrocities that happened during the next five years.

On my second day back in Nottingham I went to see Jackie's parents. I felt it was my duty to inform them of their son's fate. I would have gone to see Frank's parents also, if I had known where they lived. This is how most of the relatives of the people who died found out about their loved one's end, through friends and comrades that survived. Unfortunately, there are many that never received the truth, just the infamous telegram, 'We regret to inform you that your son is missing in action.'

With a heavy heart burdened by the truth I knocked on Mr and Mrs Wright's front door. A young girl with a slight plumpish figure answered. I took an inward breath and tried to keep any emotion from my voice. After explaining who I was I asked her, 'Are you his sister?' 'No. I'm his girlfriend,' she replied.

I was trying to look unworried and appear cheerful but I could see she looked distraught.

[Jackie was one of Erns' best friends. Ern was later to marry Betty, one of my sisters.]

I had to give them hope. I told them most of what had happened. I explained there was lots of different boats picking people up. He may have escaped and got off the ship like I did. There were many ships taking people on board, he may have been rescued on another ship.

All the time I tried to hide my real thoughts, I knew he was probably dead, he had most likely drowned. I told them I was on the ship with him and I had managed to flee before it had sunk. They were very worried, like my mum and dad had been, knowing I was still in France when it had fallen after Dunkirk. My parents did not lose their son, I knew in my swollen heart they would never see theirs again.

*Ironically, more than sixty years later I discovered
that Jackie had managed to make it off the ship
somehow, and to the shore. He died in a French
hospital about six weeks after the event. Maybe he
had inhaled or swallowed oil from the large amount
that surrounded the sinking ship. I will never
know. Recently around the sixtieth anniversary of
the loss of the Lancastria, my family and I visited
Jackie's grave in France. I was at last able to lay
a flower and say a silent prayer to my friend and
comrade Jackie Wright.*

The Commonwealth War Graves Commission website,
shows a Private 4978392 John Wright, who was 21 years
of age and served with the 2nd Battalion, The Sherwood
Foresters (Notts & Derby Regiment), and who died on
6 July 1940, which is only three weeks after the *Lancastria*
was sunk, but I believe it is the same man. His parents Walter
and Lucy Wright, lived at Hyson Green, Nottingham.

Private John Wright was buried at the Escoublac-la-
Baule War Cemetery, in the Loire-Atlantique region of
France.

*The train stopped at Southampton. We boarded
a pleasure boat named 'Gracie Fields'. It took
us across the Channel and docked at Le Havre,
near Cherbourg, part of Normandy. It was now
sometime in March. The first thing we saw was a
group of French sailors marching. When it is cold
they are allowed to march with their hands in their
pockets. This was how they were marching now.
We were disgusted, marching with their hands*

*in their pockets! Everyone remarked on this
undisciplined behaviour. Another train through
to Caen. As the train travelled through stations
the children cheered to us. We threw them biscuits
and chocolates. We could not help feeling like
heroes.*

*Their joyful voices and happy smiling faces coated
our hearts with pride. Eventually we arrived at
Rouen and we were taken to the No.1 infantry
base depot at a place named Rouvrey Woods,
a massive field or meadow completely filled with
tents, as far as I could see tents, tents and more
tents. Different regiments resided on either side
of the road.*

*A local talking point famous to the French and
the British Army was an engineer's hut situated
nearby. Apparently, this hut had changed hands
twice during the First World War, occupied by the
British and the Germans separately. They would
leave messages to each other. The story continues
in 1940, the British wrote a further message telling
the Germans to look after the hut and we were
coming back. The German reply was to thank the
British for the use of this hut. I do not know if this
is myth or truth I never saw inside the hut, then,
or after the war was over.*

*I was further excited after writing to my father
and receiving his reply. He had been stationed
in the same place during World War One, as
I now stood! He even remembered the engineer's
hut. He was part of the Royal Army Service*

*Corps (RASC). Aged 45, he drove horses taking
food and ammunition to the front line.*

*Served by the NAAFI, the food here was excellent,
and I had my first taste of tinned beans. We
ate bacon and beans, or tomatoes, on a regular
basis, like a cowboy breakfast we thought. Every
morning there was porridge and occasionally
eggs. Tinned food was in abundance during
the war. Mainly manufactured by 'Maconochy'
which came in an oval tin. However, the bread
was disgusting called 'British field bread' it was
so hard all energy had to be mustered just to chew
it. And the biscuits were worse, 'Hardbacks' they
were called. To disguise the non-sweetness of these
biscuits anything you could find was positioned on
top: cheese, bully beef, and if you were fortunate
to have margarine or butter, these also.*

*There was plenty to do here. One of the soldiers
was a skilful pianist, we would spend many an
hour singing songs, mostly dirty. Trips to the
nearby town Rouen were frequent, to their cafes
and restaurants which were not only nice places
but inexpensive. Always welcome, I tried wine and
champagne for the first time, to my distaste. I did
not drink alcohol then not even beer. My favourite
there was lemonade and citron a nice sweet drink.*

*Moreover, this was a holding camp, we were
waiting to join our regiment at the front line.
Some drill, some marching but never far from
the camp. No, at no time were we far from the
camp. Never far from my thoughts was the near*

distant future. The battle lines, the trenches, the dread. We heard rumours that events were not going our way.

One day I was sitting in one of the tents amidst the camp talking to my mates when sergeant Smith burst in. 'Somebody look at me,' he demanded, not too sharply. I was the nearest and always thought he was a nice fellow, so without much thinking I turned my head and looked up at him. 'You'll do, get your kit bag,' he ordered. Within a couple of hours, I was sat on a train along with Sergeant Smith, Corporal 'Topper' Brown, Frank Brown, Maurice Sims, Bill Wright and numerous others, about twenty in all. This was a proper train, not a cattle truck as I had previously travelled in and we were in a carriage. I felt quite privileged. But for a short while I began to worry. A pestering thought kept demanding my attention. Where we were headed for, the front line?

'I don't know where we are going, but we are going somewhere near the coast,' stated Sergeant Smith. Relief silently relaxed my tense body. We arrived at a station. 'Where are we?' Frank and I inquired. 'I think we're at Dieppe,' replied Topper Brown.

We were actually somewhere in Boulogne at a place called Reception Camp C. We still did not know the purpose for our presence here, until on parade when we were informed that a lot of troops would be passing through and we would be giving them their morning meals. This meant a prompt

4 o'clock start every morning. We were given two very comfortable huts as living quarters for this duty. Nearby was a hill, we decided to survey the surroundings. A brisk walk to the top of the hill and we could see the whole of this pleasant town, Boulogne. A further walk along the top of the hill, about 500 yards, to the cliff edge and we were rewarded with a view of dear old Blighty and the white cliffs of Dover.

The camp was run by the Pioneers. The first morning we were pleasantly surprised to be awakened by the Sergeant Major holding a bucket of tea. He was graciously known by all as Sergeant Major Tom, therefore I never discovered his surname. Every morning Sergeant Major Tom brought in that bucket of tea for us to dip in our mugs. It was lovely and extremely incredible for a man of his rank to perform such a trivial task.

After morning tea we fetched loads of tins of Maconachy stew and served them to the troops, opening tins for those with no tin openers. With the morning's assignment over we were finished for the day. As with Rouen, the townsfolk always welcomed the British troops, I suppose on account of we were fighting for their country. We stopped there for about a month and I had a lovely time with no parades, drills or marching, only a light early morning duty. We were not told of the destination of the troops passing through but discovered they may have been going to Norway.

A while after the end of the war I was talking to my cousin Arthur, his brother Tom had died in the war. I mentioned the Lancastria.

'Tom was on the Lancastria,*' he said. 'He was in the Pioneers.'*

'I thought he was a guardsman,' I inquired.

'He had to leave the guards, he was too old, he was in his forties, so he joined the Pioneers and was made a Sergeant Major.'

After another short conversation, Arthur mentioned Tom had been stationed in Boulogne. 'I was in Boulogne,' I exclaimed, 'I was in Reception Camp C.'

'He was a Sergeant Major in charge of Reception Camp C.'

'He must have been the Sergeant Major I knew there as Sergeant Major Tom.'

'Yes, it would be him.'

I was astounded, my own cousin was dear old Sergeant Major Tom. How bizarre and tragic, as he was another victim of the Lancastria.

Back at Rouen, after two to three months of sleeping in these tents, except for the month spent at Boulogne, as was the way of the army, we were marched out of the camp with no knowledge as to why. We marched to Oissel (we called it Oysel). I now know the Germans had breached the Ardennes and were in France; it was the

6th or 7th of May. We camped there for a couple of nights then marched back to the same place whence we had come. I believe there is now a British cemetery at Oissel.

On to St Nazaire

This time we were loaded on to trucks and taken back to the train station and into cattle trucks – again no information of our destination. We headed north, the way to the front line. At this moment, the time preceding every combat, especially the first time, any solder will tell you that all fears, dread, apprehensions are concentrated in the abdomen. My stomach felt like it was about to somersault. I had no need for Epsom salts. This was it. I was going into battle.

As the train continued northward no amount of cheering brought gladness to my heart. The images of war mimicked all thoughts. I could see the trenches, the guns, the cannons. The only war I knew nearer than this one, was the previous world war. My own father had been there, he had seen the abominations we were moving towards. I saw our fate through his eyes, and all the stories and history lessons that gathered to form my beliefs. The day was clear and sunny, the mood in the carriage was not. Were we all to become food for the cannons?

The train slowed as it approached a junction. A gentle tilt. It turned. It started to pick up speed. We were going South! South, back the other way.

*Away from the Germans. Slowly the truth dawned.
The rumours started to take shape. We were no
longer going in the direction of the Germans, we
were fleeing. We had heard through hearsay and
gossip that the Germans had broken through the
French lines and we had mistakenly assumed this
was tactical – a subtle method invoked to trap the
Germans advance. The new realisation pointed at
a hasty retreat. Luckily, at this time we did not
have any concept of the closeness of the enemy.*

*The ride back was contrary to the one only a
few months before. The French in their dismay
and disappointment, spat and shook their fists at
the passing carriages. This did not matter. The
sudden relief of a non-existent imminent battle
was overwhelming. Although, this was still to
come, it was in a distant future. But not as remote
as the blackness near-at-hand, the darkest day of
my life less than a week away. The last day many
of my friends and comrades would see. We were
oblivious that this path was a direct line to the
biggest British maritime disaster in history.*

*Eventually the train came to a halt at the famous
Le Mans, where the car races are held. As
I departed the train I saw the prestigious Le Mans
clock and then we actually marched along the Le
Mans Mulsanne straight. There were no cars
racing on this straight now, but thousands of men,
marching. We progressed miles and miles before
reaching a train station and boarding another
cattle truck.*

Amongst the organised bedlam, of all these men there were approximately sixty from the Sherwood Foresters, including my pals Morris, Tuggie, Bill, Jackie, Mark, Frank and Frankie. Most of the regiment had been transported to the front line before the retreat. We were on the train for a long time. Although not tightly packed, we still had to take turns to sit down. The train passed through Nantes and finally stopped at Pornichet.

The French held no grudges here and the time spent was lovely. We discovered a café run by two French girls, both a little older than us. They could speak perfect English. Their café was modelled on an English tea room, serving tea and cakes. The girls were thrilled when we commented that it looked like an English café.

After two or three days we were on the move again, this time we were ordered into single file. A line of men miles and miles long including Indians with their mules with no knowledge of the destination. Each time the man in front of you stopped, you stopped, and the man behind you stopped. A corporal belonging to my division, Taylor, a bit of a wag always making those around him laugh leaned over my shoulder. With a serious voice he spoke, 'Have you noticed there are no officers with us, there are only sergeants and sergeant majors and corporals.' I looked around me, behind and forwards realising I had not set eyes on an officer for a while. My blood boils when I think of this, they had left us behind and gone on the bloody ships long before us. I have only gleaned this in later years through conversations with others including an officer. I have no proof, but it is my belief.

It was night when we arrived at St Nazaire. We spent the night on the beach in front of a small wall. Near where we stood a monument now stands in memory of the sinking of the Lancastria. *At some time during the night, an aeroplane flew over. I have heard in later years stories of an air raid that night. I do not think so, just one plane, a shuffti kite (in Arabic, shufti to look and kite means plane). The Germans used this method to discover the strength of air raid precautions, air raid squads and guns.*

Whilst standing there a voice shouted, 'France is finished.'

'France is not finished, monsieur,' answered a defiant French soldier.

The man proclaiming France's demise was close to me, he leaned towards me and in a quieter and knowing voice said, 'France is finished.' He could speak French and had heard news bulletins on radios as we passed by the houses. He had heard France had surrendered. A shiver passed down my spine.

It was interesting to note from Jesse's story about his journey to St Nazaire. It was calm and the war, although going on around them somewhere in the distance, hadn't quite reached him and his colleagues. Maybe it was the not knowing where they were going, or why, that helped them stay relatively relaxed about matters. Even down to the fact that they had arrived the day before and then just waited.

The Sinking of the Lancastria

The next day, 17 June 1940, we continued our march, finally coming to a halt when we reached a long jetty. In the sea awaited a huge flat tender, the type used to load goods. Hundreds of soldiers boarded the tender, we were all tightly packed together as it set sail to rendezvous with the Lancastria. *We boarded the troopship* Lancastria *into one of the holds at the side of this magnificent ship; we were the last ones to come aboard. We were sent straight upstairs after being told there was no room below. We stood on the deck, starboard side, talking and looking around at the splendour of the vessel, Billy, Tuggie, Frankie, Frank, Jackie and me. A while later, I realised I was hungry. I asked the lads if they wanted anything to eat, offering bully beef and British field bread, not surprisingly they all declined so I ate the lot. A short time after swallowing the last mouthful word came round that chicken was being served down below. The rest of the lads decided to go down, 'Are you coming Mickey,' one of them asked.*

'No, I don't want anything else to eat,' I replied, 'I'll be all right.' I stood at the side of the ship looking out, my memory fails me as to whether

I was looking out to sea or inland to the river. There was a tender heading towards the ship with hundreds of squaddies on board. Someone came and stood beside me, I learned he was the boarding officer named Gratis. [This must have been Chief Officer Harry Grattidge – the names when spoken sound alike.]

He inquired, 'what is it like up the front'. I replied, 'Well, I don't know sir, I haven't a clue, we've been running all the while on trains and lorries, a bit of walking, so I couldn't tell you what happened. I don't know anything.' 'Do you know anything,' I asked. 'No, I haven't a clue,' he said.

The approaching tender was rather close now. Gratis shouted to the Captain, 'En tendre monsieur', an instruction to wait. The Captain of the Lancastria *shouted, 'what's the problem Mr Gratis.'*

'We've already got 6700 people on board. We can't possibly take any more, we're packed like sardines,' Gratis said. 'We'll just take these and that will be it, then we'll be on our way.'

I saw the number of people aboard, written down on the piece of paper he was holding. I am not entirely convinced these figures were correct. I think they were too low.

At that precise moment the first German plane appeared overhead and dropped a bomb approximately 500 yards away from us. I actually saw the second bomb leave the plane. It went over the top of us and I believe that may be the one that hit a ship nearby, the Oronsay, *hitting the bridge. In my horror and disbelief, the event seemed surreal. A few minutes later an order was given, 'everybody down below'. At the time I obeyed without question, but in hindsight this seems a daft idea. Either drown or be hit by bullets, which is worse? I had managed to go down part of the stairs when the first bomb hit us. The ship immediately tilted dangerously to the starboard side. This was when my fear was the greatest, I really thought my short life was about to end. Luckily, the ship straightened for a few minutes, giving those on the stairs a chance to scramble back onto the deck they had just left and save themselves.*

At the top of the stairs, two airmen stood, one either side of the entrance, one had a little white dog on a lead. They shouted, 'make your way to the other side of the ship,' pointing directions. Their plan was to attempt to regain the boat at an even keel, by using the weight of the passengers. It did not work, it carried on tilting more and more. Slowly and slowly as it keeled over, I clambered onto the side. By this time my fear had subsided as I planned my escape. Find anything floating in the water and swim away as fast as possible before I was sucked into the sea by the sinking ship.

As soon as the ship was flat on its side, I took all my clothes off leaving my hat until last. This was the way you would undress when going to bed. All around me others were doing the same. What a funny sight we must have looked, hundreds of naked men, except for their hats, standing there on the side of a sinking boat. A port hole opened and a pair of arms then a head appeared jutting out from it. Maurice Simms was nearby and with his and the help of two others, all four of us managed to pull out the rather weighty sergeant major. We remarkably laughed at this situation we found ourselves carrying out.

At some point my friend Jackie Wright came up to me. He was visibly scared, 'I can't swim Mickey, what shall I do?' 'Take all your clothes off, Jack, and I'll try and help you,' I instructed. 'Grab anything that floats, even if it's a dead body.' If it's floating it will hold you up, were my thoughts.

He wouldn't. He just stood there, too frightened to help himself. Sadly, I was not physically strong enough to help him, without his own assistance. I knew I had to leave the ship as quickly as possible to avoid being pulled down with it. Never a day goes by that I do not think about the friends I left behind to be claimed by the sea.

When the ship was completely flat on its side, I walked into the sea, as though I was walking from the beach. With my wallet clutched in my hand I calmly scanned the water, many kit bags and various items floated nearby, I sighted a hatch board about four feet wide directly in front of me. I put my wallet in my mouth and managed to wriggle onto the top of the board with my feet dangling in the water. I pushed myself away from the ship and started to swim as hard as I could with my feet. The board kept tipping, so I stretched out my arms wide and held onto the opposite sides to keep it steady. But I could not go very fast. I was very aware I was still in danger of the boat dragging me under, this was my only thought and the fear kept me going. I saw a plank in front of me about six inches wide and six feet long. Thinking quickly, I grabbed the plank and held it in front of me with my fingers, it slowed me down but stopped me from swaying.

Ahead I could see a destroyer, it was a long way in the distance, I decided to swim towards it. Behind me I heard the singing of 'Roll out the Barrel'. I glanced behind me; the ship was upside down. I saw men standing on it. As I swam farther away the sound of the song became more muffled with the sound of sea around me. When I looked back again the Lancastria *had vanished beneath the waves.*

It seemed like hours I was in the sea, I have no idea how long. Time passed by so slowly. Although in my vision the destroyer remained in the horizon, not really any nearer, I felt extremely lonely like I was completely on my own in the vast waters. I retained my wallet for as long as possible not wanting to lose precious pictures within, inevitably I let it go, imagining its solitary decent to the bottom of the ocean, slowly drifting downwards.

I said a silent prayer to one of my old teachers, Mrs Reynolds. Two years before leaving school she had forced me to go in the water and taught me how to swim. 'When I leave this class at the end of term, everybody in this class will be able to swim,' her voice rang. All did, except one. This was not her fault, Tommy Savage was a slow learner, a really nice lad but slow to learn anything.

Onwards I continued, the water lashing around me. Complete solitude. My legs becoming weaker, but I continued to kick.

Eventually a rowing boat came into view in front of me. Aboard were two Frenchmen a fisherman and his son, a soldier. They pulled me into the boat. One of my mates, Peter Moore, appeared on the other side of the craft. He was also in the Army and lived only a few miles from me in Sneinton. I will be eternally grateful to those two Frenchmen. Pete and I sat in the front as they rowed to the destroyer I had been heading for. There was no room for anybody else in the boat.

On reaching the destroyer, we said our good-byes and thanks to our two saviours and clambered up the netting on the side of the ship. I noticed the name of the ship under the bell, Haverock, *a H class, H44. As we neared the top sailors pulled us onto the deck. We were both covered in oil that had spewed from the damaged ship. Sailors took us below deck to the showers. One of them stated, 'you both look more like a blackboard and easel'. It took a long time to remove all the oil, some had to be scrapped off. This did not matter, I was saved, no longer in any danger but in a nice hot shower. Years later one of my daughters wondered if I was not frightened being on board another ship so soon after the disaster. 'No,' I replied 'I felt safe, I was with The Navy.'*

As I had no clothes, I was given a blanket. With it wrapped around me I was sent upstairs to a room furnished with chairs and tables. I think it was one of the mess rooms. Occupying the room were a couple of men, some children, two women who were possibly nurses, and other squaddies including Maurice Simms, Taylor (the wag) and Peter Moore. We swapped stories of escaping the doomed ship, talking to different people. Several had left the ship in lifeboats or some other sort of boat.

Sometime later a petty officer entered the room, 'got something to eat for you down below'. I was the nearest to him, 'Ok,' I answered. 'You don't need your blanket,' he stated. Feeling embarrassed, having to admit I was sitting here with no clothes on in the presence of women and children, I tried to answer discreetly, lowering my voice. 'I do, I haven't got any clothes on.'

'Are you naked?' he inquired.

'Yes, I can't take this off with women here.'

'Hang on a bit, come with me,' he gestured.

He took me to another part of the boat and gave me a pair of his trousers. He shouted to one of the Jacktars (sailors) for a coat, he brought me a sailor's jersey and that is what I wore until we arrived at Blighty.

We had a meal as it was beginning to grow dark. I figured I must have been in the water for several hours. The ship commenced its journey home. When I awoke the next morning I heard a cry that we were at anchor at Devonport. We docked at a sailors' station, HMS Drake. These ports are often named like this. Throughout the war the Germans have amusingly made claims to sinking HMS Drake twice and also HMS Arthur which was a port at Skegness. On departing the Haverock *I noticed the other ship to be bombed near the coast of St Nazaire, the* Oronsay *was already anchored at Devonport.*

We survivors were treated wonderfully here. I was examined by a doctor. 'How are you feeling?' he asked. 'I am feeling a bit tight around here,' pointing to my chest, 'I don't know why.'

'Probably the oil,' he answered, 'you probably breathed a lot of fumes in. You can smell it anyway.'

I was not aware how bad the disaster was. Weeks later I read in the papers, 2,500 saved with 2,000 dead. I knew that was a monstrous lie. I had heard the boarding officer, Mr Gratis, seen his papers. With only 2,500 survivors I knew the loses were at least twice that many.

There were 2,477 known survivors of the sinking of the *Lancastria*, and according to Jesse Fenton, he had seen the figure of 6,700 on the boarding officer's sheet of paper, and there were about 100 men on the flat tender full of men, who were the last ones to embark before the *Lancastria* set sail. This takes the figure to those on board to approximately 6,800. Take away the 2,477 survivors and that means 4,323, men, women and children perished as a result of the *Lancastria* being bombed by the Luftwaffe and the ship sinking. The Commonwealth War Graves Commission website records the names of 1,482 military personnel who were killed on 17 June 1940, along with four members of the Merchant Navy, who were either buried in France or who had their names commemorated on war memorials there.

If all the above figures are correct, that would mean 2,837 civilian men, women and children perished with the sinking of the *Lancastria*.

Back to Jesse's story.

I never looked back, we were at war, no time to dwell on the past. It was years later before the full realisation of the tragedy struck me. Delayed shock I think they call it now. Although I thought about my friends, I had not spared a moment's thought for all those other men, women and children trapped inside as the ship went down. Some burned alive, some injured, some unhurt but unable to escape. How lucky I was and how sad all those young lads lost their lives. I remember them as young lads.

I thought of all the ones trapped below, feeling empathetic to their horror, I believed I was trapped for a moment, until the ship regained an even keel. I could understand their last trepidation before oblivion. All those people on top of the ship, my friend I had to leave behind, all gone in a hideous death. Could I have done more to help Jackie? I know in my heart I was not a strong enough swimmer, there was nothing more I could have done, but still, the question lingers. At times I experience a down hearted feeling, especially when I recollect Jackie Wright. I even spare a thought for the little white dog; did it manage to escape with its master? They were on the top of the ship, it is possible. I feel angry when I think of the officers who went on ahead, probably taking the lifejackets. They could most likely swim and had a chance to escape. Not like Jackie and the rest of them left stranded, singing, on top of the mighty Lancastria.

A really enthralling and detailed, personal account of not only what happened immediately before, during, and after the sinking of the *Lancastria*, but one that included his war time involvement, and his thoughts and feelings on the matter many years after they had taken place.

CHAPTER 7

James William Arthur Burke's Story

Whilst researching this book I made contact with Mrs Dierdre Hill, whose grandfather, Sergeant 1417330 James William Arthur Burke, served with the Royal Artillery attached to the Headquarters 12th Anti-Aircraft Brigade, during the Second World War, and was a victim of the sinking of the SS *Lancastria*.

James Burke was an extremely interesting character, born on 6 February 1903, he initially enlisted in the Army during the First World War on 1 April 1919, when he was only 16 years of age. He became a Gunner (210732) in the Royal Garrison Artillery, but he only served for 271 days before being discharged on 27 December 1919, for being too young to undertake military service. However, he was not to be deterred and on 12 February 1920, when he had reached the age of 17 years and 6 days, he enlisted again at Whitehall in London, when he signed on for a term of twelve years – eight years with the colours and four years on the Army Reserve.

His time in the Army saw him serve in Mesopotamia between 1 May 1920 until 4 January 1921. The journey out there took forty-three days and the return journey took thirty-two. He also served in Turkey between 30 September 1922 and 26 August 1923, with an additional twenty days added to this time for travelling there and back.

At the time of the completion of his eight years' service on 11 February 1928, he was a Gunner (1417330) with the 1st Medium Brigade, Royal Artillery, and it was then that he was placed on the Army Reserve. Having subsequently spent four years on the Army Reserve, James was discharged from the Army on 11 February 1932 at the Woolwich Barracks in London having completed his twelve years' service with the British Army. His service saw him awarded the General Service Medal.

Although James had been a 'fitter's mate' before he joined the Army, after having been transferred on to the Army Reserve, his Army Service record shows that on returning to civilian life, he became a servant. It also shows that his military conduct was exemplary, and that the final assessment of his character on leaving the Army was as follows:

> *An excellent type of man who has completed 8 years of service without a single entry against him. An efficient and hardworking clerk with a good memory. Always obliging, cheerful and reliable. He is a good officer servant and does not drink or smoke.*

I believe that most people would be more than happy at having such words written about their character and personality, on such an official document.

James was a married man. The wedding to his sweetheart, Valentine Elliot, took place at the Catholic

Church in Shoeburyness on 10 August 1926. James was 23 years of age and Valentine was 20. At the time, James was already serving as a bombardier in the Royal Artillery and was stationed at Shoeburyness Barracks, near Southend. Valentine's home address is recorded on the wedding certificate as being the Staff House at Shoeburyness Barracks, which, I would suggest, is how they came to meet.

James didn't wait to be called up for service during the Second World War, instead he enlisted in the British Army on 3 May 1939 at Stonebridge Park in North West London. At the time he was 36 years of age. He was posted as a gunner to the Royal Artillery.

Having spent five months undergoing his basic training, he was sent out to France as part of the British Expeditionary Force on 13 October 1939, before returning home to England on 10 January 1940; but just ten days later he was back in France, suggesting that it was a period of leave.

As the Battle for France was drawing to a close and its inevitable outcome, James was one of the British soldiers who had been sent to St Nazaire for evacuation back to the UK. On arrival at the port he would have most probably had to have waited in a tented camp in the fields that surrounded the port. When it was his turn, he would have been instructed to make his way down to the port with his colleagues, and then ferried by a small tender the mile and a half out to sea where the *Lancastria* was waiting at anchor. How long he was on board before the bombs struck, or whereabouts he was on the ship, are not known.

James survived the actual sinking of the vessel, but having been rescued, died later the same day on board the HMT *Oronsay*, of double pneumonia and injuries sustained as a result of the subsequent bombing and sinking of the *Lancastria*.

Although he died whilst on board the *Oronsay* he does not have a grave as he was buried at sea, though it would have only been a matter of a few hours before the *Oronsay* reached the port on the south coast of England. His name is commemorated on the Dunkirk Memorial in the Nord Region of France.

On 17 June 1940, the day that the *Lancastria* was sunk, Valentine, who was commonly known by her middle name of Mena, sent a letter to James, totally unaware of the set of circumstances which had already resulted in his death. Mena's address is shown on the letter as being 'Sudbury', Canewdon Road, Ashingdon, Near Rochford, Essex.

My own darling,

I was so pleased to receive even a card dated 11th from you this morning, although I was hoping for a letter.

The news today seems very grave and I am wondering now what will happen to you who are left over there. George tried to cheer me by saying it will mean you coming back here. I can only go on hoping you are safe my darling and trust in God to bring you back to us.

I had just got back from the shops this morning when George brought Jess and Rita down to see me, he went on his journey and left Jess here for the day. I was so glad to have her and wonder she does not come more often. We had a cup of tea, and all walked back with her, and had our tea up her place. The girls and George were getting ready to go to a dance, which seemed all wrong to my idea, when others are fighting for their lives. Certainly, it seems to them that they are doing their best, for Jessie was to play her accordion and the proceeds were to go for the troops.

The boys had great fun in the field, George had cut his grass for hay making and they had high jinks. We walked back after the nine o'clock news, and they were all very tired, and soon in bed and asleep, but I could not sleep. My heart aches for you and my longing seems unbearable, more so now for I don't know where you are, or what has become of you, and the awful dread that we might never see you again, but something tells me to have faith and go on hoping.

I'm going to bed now, not to sleep my brain is too much turmoil, but to rest for a while. My thoughts are always with you darling and your name on my lips praying for your return.

God bless you my darling and keep you safe. We all wish you good luck and try to keep smiling.

George said tonight the darkest cloud has a silver lining, so we must go on looking for it.

Good night my love.

> *Ever yours loving Mena, write soon*
> *Patsy x Peter x Michael x Robert.*

Mena wrote another letter to James dated Wednesday 19 June. In it she sounded quite calm and spoke mainly of home and the day to day goings on at home. She wrote a further letter the following day, on Thursday 20 June, and the tone of the writing has changed dramatically.

> *My own Darling,*
>
> *No letter from you again and I am getting so worried and anxious, as it's been given out on the wireless, that the BEF has come back to England, and I feel if you could, you would write to me at once. I spoke to a woman today who heard yesterday from her husband to say he was back in England, and I feel more anxious than ever now. The last letter I received from you was dated the 10th and today is the 20th and so much has happened between those days.*
>
> *Patsy does not seem at all well since Tuesday and I think she is worrying inwardly about you as much as I am, although she does not say much, she never did, as you know.*
>
> *Thank you for the sweet little rose, I would like to have seen the lovely garden. I wonder if it's still as lovely and is the dear old lady safe. Have enclosed a little rose in return, for you, it is the first of ours to bloom. The boys took their tea to school today and those belonging to life boys were going for a picnic not far away, they had to take their cups and sugar and a lady was lending her garden for the occasion and making tea for them. They were very excited about going. Patsy and*

I had our tea in the garden, and just after we had finished, Loui Haysman came over and asked if Patsy could have tea with her, so she went over to play with her for a while.

Now my darling I have no more news for you this time but hope to soon have news from you that will relieve my mind. We have been putting paper strips in the windows, some job, still have two more to do.

Keep smiling and hoping for the best as I try to do. We are thinking of you all the time darling, and longing to see you, and my love for you is greater than ever.

God bless you dear and keep you safe always. Fond love from us all.

Ever your own.

Mena, Patsy, Peter, Michael, Robert.

It is sad to think that this letter was written some two days after James was dead. A letter so beautifully worded, filled with love and affection and one that James never received.

James's wife, Valentine, did not receive the telegram informing her that he was dead, until 28 June 1940, and when it arrived, Mena, read it, slipped it in to her pocket, and carried on making dinner for her four children, clearly not wanting any of them to see her in tears. The content of it is as follows.

(Burke Sudbury) Canewden Road, Ashingdon, Rochford, Essex. Deeply regret to inform you

1417330 Burke, James William, killed on board troopship 17/6/40.

Having seen a copy of the actual telegram that James's wife, Valentina, received, informing her of his death, what struck me the most about it is the minimal number of words which it contains. I appreciate that it was only intended as a notification of death to the next of kin, but the effect that must have had on Valentina would have been colossal. Imagine, being at home, alone, or just in the company of young children, and you get a knock on the door to find out it's the postman with a telegram. It would be enough to make your heart miss a beat.

On 12 July 1940, Valentina received the following typed letter from a second lieutenant serving with the 12th Anti-Aircraft Brigade, Drill Hall, Tadcaster, Yorkshire.

Dear Mrs Burke,

Your letter dated 26th June 1940 addressed to the Commander of this Brigade, has been handed to me to answer as I was the officer in charge of the personnel of this Brigade HQ who were evacuated from France by SS Lancastria. Your husband Sgt Burke, was amongst these, and he was definitely on board the ship when she was sunk by enemy action at St Nazaire on June 17th.

During the journey home on a ship which had taken aboard some hundreds of survivors, I personally made enquiries of all the 12th AA Brigade HQ personnel who knew your husband, as to whether they had seen anything of him after the disaster. At that time no one knew anything at all definite, and the only information I can give you at all about him is that he was seen below decks shortly after the ship was struck.

I very much fear, as we have had no news of him since, that he, among many others, must have been lost with the ship, but it is impossible to say exactly how. This is one of the really sad features of a disaster of this kind. There is always a faint possibility that he may, somehow or other, been rescued, or found his way on wreckage to the French coast. As this is now in enemy hands, it is of course impossible to check up in any way or make enquiries. I feel it only right to tell you, however, as one of the survivors, that I consider this only a very faint possibility, and I do not think you should build up any hope of your husband's survival.

This will be poor comfort to you in your bereavement, but I feel that I should say that your husband was much liked by his comrades, and his officers at all times found him glad and willing to take on any job that wanted doing.

Your husband's comrades and the officers of this HQ offer you their heartfelt sympathy and should we at any time hear any more of what happened to him, we will not fail to communicate with you.

Yours faithfully
2nd Lieutenant, Royal Artillery
Acting Staff Captain
12th AA Brigade.

A letter dated 9 November 1940, sent from the Royal Artillery Records Office, The Minories, London, EC.3, to Mrs Valentine Burke, at 'Sudbury', Canewdon Road, Ashingdon, Rochford, read as follows.

Dear Mrs Burke,

I am to inform you that further enquiries have been made into the death of your husband the late No.1417330 War Sergeant James William BURKE, and the information I have received is as follows.

He did not die on board His Majesty's 'Lancastria' on the 17th June 1940 as previously stated, but was transferred to his Majesty's Troop Ship 'Oronsay' where on the night of 17/18th June 1940, he died from severe wounding and double pneumonia contracted as the result of enemy action.

I have been in touch with the Army Chaplain who was with him at the time of his death, and he states that he did not suffer much before his death.

He was buried by the same Army Chaplain at sea on 18th June 1940. I have been asked to inform you that he was very well looked after and that he died peacefully in the presence of many of his comrades.

I am dear Madam
Your obedient Servant
J.G.L. Cowie
(For Colonel)

Above left: Ernest Beesley, survivor of the sinking of the *Lancastria*, when he was 99 years of age.

Above right: Ernest Beesley.

Above left: John Glackin, a survivor of the sinking of the *Lancastria*.

Above right: Private John Ames - Survivor of the sinking of the *Lancastria*.

Above: Post card of the *Lancastria*.

Left: *Lancastria* before the war.

Above left: The *Lancastria's* bell at St Catherine Cree Church in London.

Above right: Lancastria Memorial, Liverpool.

A Junkers aircraft that sunk the *Lancastria*.

Right: The *Lancastria* leaving port.

Below: Memorial in Saint-Nazaire.

Left: Cunard Line post card of the *Lancastria*.

Below: The *Lancastria* sinking.

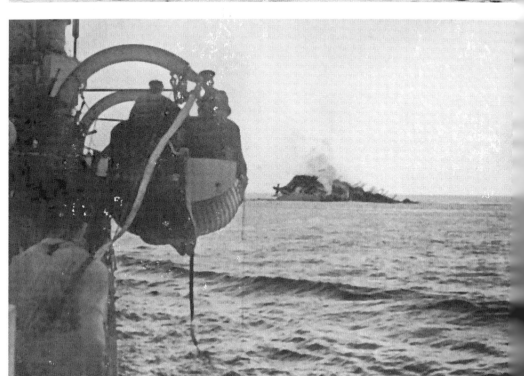

The *Lancastria*, sinking off St Nazaire.

Evacuees from the *Lancastria*.

Above: *Lancastria* survivors.

Right: Jesse Fenton.

Sinking of the Lancastria.

Medal issued by Scottish Government, for survivors or their families.

Below are two undated letters which were written to Mena by a friend and colleague of her husband, Sergeant 6630045 Hepburn, who served with the 158th/53rd Heavy Anti-Aircraft Brigade, Royal Artillery, and who worked with him before they embarked on the *Lancastria* and was on board the vessel when it was attacked and sunk.

Dear Mrs Burke

I am writing in answer to a letter from the 12th AA Brigade, which was sent to me, asking to let you know about your husband, who was a great pal of mine in France. Well, all I can tell you is that we were together until our ship got bombed, but just before, I said to him that I was going to have a bath, and I was in it when the ship got struck. When I got out I saw him going down to his cabin. I called out to him and he said he would not be long, because at that time we were all lining up waiting the order to go up top, but as you have read, it was every man for himself. That was the last I saw of him. But still, never give up hope, because where we are, men are still turning up, because all of us went different ways, and let's hope he got back to France. If so, he will be kept there until after the end of the war, so keep your chin up and hope for the best.

From
George A. Hepburn.

The second letter read as follows.

Just a few lines to let you know how sorry I am in not answering your letter sooner, but you will have to excuse me, because the letter arrived whilst I was on leave, that made it seven days late before I got it, and to make it later still, on returning back off leave, the battery had moved, so do not think I have forgotten to write to you, because where we are now there is not much tim, because we are having a rough time, but that is our job.

Well, I can tell you what happened between the dates you refer to, and it was then we left Rheims and arrived at a place called St Nazaire, where we were for a week, but we could not write any letters home, but we had the pleasure of writing a field card, which we both wrote home. But things were getting a bit hot so we had to move again, and we arrived at a place called Nuan. Once again, the post was bad, but we wrote a letter hoping they would get home, and what's more I don't think they got home. We were there until the 15th of June, and once again we were off, to a place called Nantes, but we only had one night there, because on the following morning we went on to the place where we got the boat, and that is what happened from those dates, but as I mention in my first letter, still keep up hope, as you never know what will turn up.

Hoping from the bottom of my heart you will be one of the lucky ones that we read of daily. So cheers and all the very best of luck.

From Sgt Hepburn.

I wonder if Sergeant Hepburn was being totally honest with Mena about his personal thoughts, or whether he was simply trying to keep her hopes up, as would be normal in such cases. But having said that, with so much doubt about what happened to an individual, there was always a certain amount of hope until someone came up with an unarguable, factual explanation about what had actually happened to James Burke.

On 22 August 1940, James Burke's widow, Mena, wrote a letter to his mother at her home Ashingdon, near Rochford, Southend. Now in itself the letter offers nothing new to the sinking of the *Lancastria*, but what it does do is offer an insight in to how the relatives of those who had lost loved ones in the tragedy, dealt initially with the uncertainty of the situation and then the knowledge that they were not actually going to see their loved ones ever again.

When I first read the letter I was uncertain as to how I was going to include it in this book. It was Deirdre Hill, who sent me a copy of that letter and in response, I asked her how she felt it directly connected to the sinking of the *Lancastria*. In reply, she said the following: 'Mena (her grandmother) had written this to Jim's (James') mother. By this time, Mena realised James was not coming back, but had still not fully accepted what had happened.'

Once I read that, I fully understood the true worth of the letter. This is two months after the sinking of the *Lancastria,* and the reality is that she will not know if James is dead or alive until she receives the official confirmation letter on 9 November. She hasn't heard anything official about her husband. He could have been wounded and sent to hospital. He could have been picked up by a French boat, who with the belief that German troops would imminently be arriving in St Nazaire, took him to a place of safety. He could have been captured by the Germans and taken as a prisoner of war, or he could have been killed. The truth is that when Mena wrote that letter to James's mother, she didn't know with any degree of certainty exactly what had happened to her husband. With this in mind, the fact that she was able to write a five page letter to her mother-in-law, showing concern for her and her circumstances, whilst at the same time dealing with her own worst fears and as well as keeping up a brave front for the sake of her four children, makes the letter even more remarkable. Here is what she wrote:

> *'Sudbury', Canewdon Road*
> *Ashingdon*
> *Nr Rochford, Essex*

My Dear Mum,

Was so relieved to get your letter this morning and to know you are alright, for I have worried a great deal about you knowing you had had pretty severe raids that way. I have a friend living at 'Eastleigh', no doubt you can call her to mind, 'Mrs Hooper' who we had rooms with when we were at Larkhill. I had a letter from her this week, she says the raids have been awful that way, and dog fights overhead almost every day. That is just outside Southampton isn't it? We have had many scares, and bombs have been dropped at Barling, the next village to mum. They did not explode and did little damage. Shoeburyness has had it pretty bad I hear.

My brother Tom and his wife gave me an unexpected visit Sunday after dinner when the children were getting ready for Sunday school but the all-clear went just after. I was just getting tea ready when the alarm went again and we heard planes, one of the kiddies ran in and said 42 planes were up, we went to the back of our garden and watched and more and more came over from out of the clouds. They passed along and my neighbours said they must be ours or the guns would fire at them. Then we saw one catch fire and the pilot took to his parachute and we all got so excited thinking it was an enemy, then I thought, 'poor man, he has left someone over there who loves him'.

Those last couple of lines are quite possibly a reflection of the turmoil that Mena was experiencing herself at the time. Two months after the *Lancastria* had been sunk, and she still didn't know for certain whether her husband James was alive or dead. The letter continued:

We heard after, it was one of our own planes and the poor chap landed in the river mud. If the tide had been up he would have drowned. His goggles caught fire and he was badly burned, and I think he has lost his sight. How terrible it all is and what a blessing it will be to have peace again. I look forward to before the end comes, I have had the worst blow they could give me, but there are still my little kids and I pray God will protect them, and all of you I love, from this awful terror.

So glad to hear Will will not be too far from home and hope he will be lucky enough to have a good billet. Also pleased to hear Alice and little ones are well. I expect they miss their daddy.

When Mena talks about Alice, and the little ones missing their daddy, is she really talking about herself and her own four children? It is noticeable that after writing about how her friends' children must be feeling, her thoughts then immediately turn to her husband.

I had a letter from Jim's pal who was with him in France and I have enclosed it for you to read. The officer who wrote sent him a stamped envelope and asked him to write to me which I thought very kind of him. You know mum, I can't think our Jim has gone sometimes. I feel he must come back and I must go on hoping that one day he will, or I think I will go mad.

Well dear, the insurance has not been settled yet and I'm wondering if there are reasons why it is taking so long. I had my papers through this week about my pension, it will be £2-10-3 a week which is not so bad, I thought I would not have enough to manage on, and work here is a job to get without going into town, and would mean leaving the children all day. The allowances for children are paid up to 16 years of age. There does not seem much chance of getting a cheaper place. I asked my agent if the landlord would lower the rent, and I had a letter back to say they would accept 14/- a week for the duration of the war, that's 1/6 off and is better than 1/6 on, and will pay my electric light.

Peter was very pleased with his little note and I expect he will write to you soon.

My mum and dad came over Tuesday to see us and they had quite a nice time with us. They brought us some potatoes, carrots, apples and plums from their garden. When the raid alarm sounded we had the wireless on and did not hear it. The young man next door called and told us. We heard big explosions in the distance and the children did not come out of school for an hour after their usual time. They keep them there until the all clear goes.

I'm pleased to say they are all well, they are all very brave and seem to have no fear, which is a very good thing. I would rather have them like that than terrified, after all there's nothing any of us can do about it, only trust in God to bring us safely through.

Fondest love to you and Auntie Gertrude from us all. Ever your loving daughter, Mena.

Hope you soon have news from Ernie and I know how anxious you must be. Mum has not heard from O.

What an amazing letter for Mena to be able to write at such a difficult time in her own life. She must have been an incredibly strong individual, who had to deal with all of her own issues surrounding the uncertainty of whether James was alive or dead, whilst holding down a job, bringing up four young children, keeping a roof over their heads, and also finding time to show concern and worry for her mother-in-law and other extended family members.

CHAPTER 8

Ernest Beesley

On 30 November 2016, when *Lancastria* survivor Ernest Beesley was 99 years of age, I interviewed him in the care home where he lives in Uxbridge. A lovely old fashioned gentleman, who it was an absolute pleasure to meet, I only spent a couple of hours in his company, but what an experience it was as he told me all about his military service during the Second World War and surviving the sinking of the *Lancastria* on 17 June 1940.

Ernest Beesley was born in Wallingford on 30 September 1917 and during the Second World War he served in the Royal Engineers. He was conscripted in October 1939 and was eventually called up in January 1940, to become a Sapper (1923731) in the 149th Railway Construction Company, Royal Engineers. Having been in the Army for just seven weeks he found himself being sent out to France as part of the British Expeditionary Force sometime at the end of May 1940. Ernest and his colleagues sailed from Southampton to Le Havre, after which they had to endure a three hour train journey which took them to a camp somewhere between Nantes and St Nazaire, but Ernest couldn't recall its name. There they had to carry out work on the railways and build railway sidings, the purpose of which was to help store ammunition should the need occur.

They had only been at the camp for about three weeks, when they were told to pack up all of their kit, belongings and equipment, as they were on the move. They climbed aboard a number of Army trucks and off they went. Their unknown destination turned out to be fields just outside St Nazaire, where they ended up staying for ten days. On 17 June 1940 they were driven down to the port, and in groups of forty, they climbed on board a small tender and were taken a mile and a half out to sea where the *Lancastria* was at anchor.

Ernest was with a friend of his by the name of Bert Bacon. As the tender pulled alongside the *Lancastria*, they climbed up the side of the ship and once on deck were met with an announcement by the captain over the tannoy: *'Anyone just joining the ship, please make yourselves as comfortable as possible on deck, as there is no more room down below. Those wanting or in need of a sea water shower can do so in the ship's hold.'*

Having had his much needed shower, Ernest made his way back up on deck. He had only been there for a few minutes when the first of the bombs struck the *Lancastria*. 'It shook and shuddered,' Ernest said. 'I didn't know what was happening at first, but it quickly became apparent that we had been hit.' Ernest didn't panic, he didn't have time to. He and his friend Bert were at the back of the ship by the anchor, far enough away from the explosion not to have been wounded and were on the shore side. Fortunately there were a number of life jackets near to where they were standing, nothing substantial, cork-based ones that had a number of pouches, but better than nothing, especially for those who couldn't swim. Bert couldn't swim but for some reason he wouldn't put the life jacket on, and the next thing Ernest knew was Bert had run off to another part of the ship. Ernest had already made up his mind about what he was going to do, so he slid into his life jacket, tightened it as best he could and jumped into the sea. 'I was a good swimmer,' he said, 'So I jumped in. I swam for about half a mile, and by now the surface of the water was awash with oil that had escaped from the *Lancastria*.'

Ernest then explained how he was spotted by a Royal Naval corvette. As the vessel pulled up alongside him, one of the crew checked that he wasn't wounded, and threw him a rubber raft that had enough room for six men. That number was quickly achieved and it wasn't long before another ten men were hanging on to the sides. After a while Ernest got cramp in one of his legs and stood up, but in doing so, he lost his balance, fell into the water and was unable to get back on to the raft. He started to swim back towards the shore, when he came across a rowing boat that was making its way towards the *Lancastria*. 'Can you row?' enquired an officer. 'Yes, I should think so.' Before he knew it, he was in the small boat rowing as fast as he could towards the *Lancastria* to pick up as many survivors as possible. The officer didn't want to get too close to the stricken vessel just in case she sank and dragged the small rowing boat down with her. Having picked up a few survivors Ernest started rowing towards the shore, but before reaching there, the corvette that had thrown him the life raft, came alongside and picked Ernest and the others up and took them to the nearby troopship, the *Oronsay,* which then made its way back to England, docking at Plymouth.

Ernest and those with him were taken to an 'isolation' camp not too far from the harbour. There they were documented, fed and clothed. After a few days of sleeping and relaxing each man was given three weeks leave to go home and visit their families, and reminded not to talk to anybody, friend or family, about what had happened aboard the *Lancastria.*

Ernest's is the only account I have heard where someone has stated that they were told not to talk to anybody about their experience on board the ship. Of all the newspaper articles and personal accounts that started appearing in the British Press, not one of them mentioned being told not to talk about their experiences concerning the sinking of the *Lancastria,* although I have no doubt that such an order was given to all survivors.

With the three weeks up, Ernest re-joined his unit. About forty of them were sent to Barnet to help the railway staff with repairing the town's bomb-damaged railway station. After that task was completed, they remained in and around the London area carrying out similar work at other bomb-damaged railway stations. Whilst doing this work, it wasn't unusual for Ernest and his comrades to find themselves in the middle of an air raid and when that happened they had to find cover as best they could. At Lambeth, they hid under the nearby arches whilst the Germans were dropping their bombs.

Ernest ended up at a makeshift camp halfway between Oxford and Banbury, where a siding had been added to the main line right next to three big lakes. The reason for this was so that all of the wartime rubble in and around the south of England could be dumped in it. With the siding in place a train could just back up and deposit its load of bricks, masonry, wood and concrete directly into the lake. Most of the loads were in the region of 10 tons.

On 1 September 1941, Ernest and his comrades were all sent to be vaccinated and despite not being told why, it didn't take a genius to work out that the chances of them remaining in England were slim.

As if not busy enough, Ernest's life managed to get even busier during the final few months of the year. On 1 October 1941 he married his sweetheart Doris at Ealing Registry Office followed by a two-week honeymoon at Truro in the west country where his sisters had been evacuated. On 11 November, the newly wed Ernest was sent up to Stoke-on-Trent on a bridging course, where he was taught to make heavy duty bridges that were capable of taking the weight of military vehicles such as tanks. After completing the course, which lasted a few weeks, they found themselves on a lorry and on their way to Liverpool Docks where they embarked on the SS *Duchess of Bedford*, which had been built for the Canadian Pacific Steamships Company in 1928, but had been commandeered by the Admiralty at the outbreak of the Second World War.

Despite Ernest's previous experience of being a 'passenger' on a troop ship, the SS *Lancastria,* he had absolutely no qualms about getting on board the *Duchess of Bedford*, although he couldn't help but notice that some of his louder and somewhat gregarious comrades, were noticeably a lot quieter than they usually were.

'We never knew where we were going. Nobody ever told us. We only ever found out where we were going when we got there,' Ernest said with a wry smile on his face. 'That's just how it was I suppose.'

The *Duchess of Bedford* made its way out of Liverpool, into the Irish Sea, then the Atlantic Ocean, before ending up at Freetown in Sierra Leone, where she remained at anchor for about a week whilst waiting for a convoy, before continuing on to Durban where they arrived on 12 December 1941. This was less than a week after the Japanese had attacked the American Fleet at Pearl Harbor in Hawaii, news that Ernest and his colleagues were not aware of.

The plan had been to spend Christmas in Durban, but after going to sleep on Christmas Eve, Ernest woke up on Christmas day to find the *Duchess of Bedford* at sea in the Indian Ocean, and although he didn't know it at the time, they were on their way to Bombay, India. Once there, they disembarked and made their way to the Royal Berkshire peace time barracks. 'By the time we arrived at the barracks we were all absolutely knackered. It was a long march from the port to the barracks. We didn't even undress or take our boots off, we just climbed into our rope beds and went to sleep.'

Ernest couldn't recall exactly how long they were in Bombay, but when the *Duchess of Bedford* left the city in a convoy on 9 January 1942, he moved to the USS *West Point*, which Ernest described as being a 'beautiful ship'. Before the war she had been the SS *America,* an ocean liner built in 1940 for the United States Lines.

The *West Point* was too big to dock alongside any of the piers in the harbour at Bombay, so the men had to embark upon lighters and smaller vessels and brought alongside the *West Point*, to be able to get on board. The convoy, which consisted of the *West Point,* the *Wakefield,* the three British transport ships, the *Duchess of Bedford,*

Empress of Japan and the *Empire Star,* all left in convoy. The *West Point* was carrying a total of 5,272 military personnel, which included Ernest, but why he didn't continue on board the *Duchess of Bedford,* isn't clear. The convoy was well protected on her journey down to Singapore, with an escort of three cruisers and four destroyers. But despite this protection there were major concerns about the presence of Japanese submarines in the area of the Indian archipelago, which was part of the route that the Allied convoy was due to sail through. To ensure the convoy's safety, a 200-mile detour was taken so that the ships could sail through the shallower waters and coral studded Sunda Straits between Java and Sumatra.

Ernest remarked that once on board the *West Point,* they were given lectures about the Japanese, which surprised him somewhat, because although he had been aware of the Japanese attack on Pearl Harbor, prior to leaving Durban, it had never crossed his mind that they might become involved with fighting them.

On 29 January 1942 Ernest arrived at Singapore aboard the *West Point,* but they didn't dock at the island's massive British built naval base due to the fact that by then it was having to endure daily Japanese air raids. Instead they proceeded to Keppel Harbour where commercial vessels docked. Once there the *West Point* off loaded supplies, equipment and American troops. The only ones who remained on board were Ernest and his 669 comrades from the Royal Engineers.

Because of the sporadic nature of the Japanese air raids across Singapore at that time, the unloading of equipment and supplies took a lot longer than had been anticipated, so the Royal Engineers, members of the crew, and twenty-two local workers, were tasked with getting the job done.

The *West Point* commander, Captain Lewis, had a meeting with British authorities in Singapore the outcome of which was that he agreed to take on board a thousand women and children, and such additional men as the British deemed necessary, and to convey all of them to Ceylon (Sri Lanka).

Ernest was amongst those tasked with standing guard at the bottom of *West Point's* 'gang plank' checking the passes of those leaving and joining the vessel. Once that was done they assisted the wives and children of British naval personnel who had been stationed at the island's naval base, to embark with their luggage and show them to their cabins.

After completing the loading of those who were being evacuated, preparations for departure were begun. But that final day, 30 January 1942, was certainly an eventful one. More than thirty Japanese aircraft carried out attacks in Keppel Harbour. Several bombs fell close to HMS *Exeter,* which had a lucky escape when two bombs landed one either side of the vessel, with thankfully no damage being caused or any injuries sustained. The American vessel, *Wakefield*, wasn't so fortunate. She took a direct hit to her forward section, which resulted in her sick bay being destroyed, killing five and wounding a further nine. A small tanker that was moored close to the *West Point* was struck by a bomb dropped by a Japanese aircraft and sunk.

At 1800 hours on 30 January 1942 the *West Point*, with Ernest Beesley one of the 1,276 men, women and children on board, left Singapore on the way to Ceylon.

The comparison between Ernest's escape from St Nazaire and Singapore, are so similar, that it is worthy of mention, to show the type of man that Ernest is. To have survived the sinking of the *Lancastria,* would have mentally scarred many, especially with the number of people who were believed killed. Although he had no choice on being embarked on the *Duchess of Bedford* or the *West Point*, undertaking the journey from Liverpool to Singapore via Durban and Bombay, took some courage, especially as just sixteen days after leaving Singapore Lieutenant General Arthur Ernest Percival surrendered all military personnel on the island to Japanese forces under the command of General Tomoyuki Yamashita.

In Singapore he once again found himself on board a cruise liner used for military purposes to evacuate troops and civilians from a war zone whilst being bombed by enemy aircraft. At St Nazaire he was evacuated just eight days before the fall of France to Nazi Germany, and at Keppel harbour in Singapore he was evacuated sixteen days before the island was surrendered to the Japanese. There cannot be many British soldiers who served in the Second World War who experienced two such similar events.

When I interviewed Ernest in November 2016, I did not ask him what was going through his mind in Singapore when the *West Point,* along with other Allied vessels, was being attacked from the air at Keppel harbour, but I would imagine it would have been something like, 'Oh no. Not again.'

Ernest was a very brave young man during his years of service during the Second World War. There are those who would have been understandably mentally broken by their experience of surviving the sinking of the *Lancastria,* but he picked himself up, dusted himself down, and got on with the job in hand. To then survive a carbon copy of that incident and still come out of it in one piece is a remarkable achievement. As I approach the completion of writing this book, Ernest is just three months away from reaching his 102nd birthday, and he still has a smile on his face and a twinkle in his eye.

CHAPTER 9

The Story of John Glackin

Whilst researching for this book I discovered the name of Bernadette Glackin, whose late father, John Glackin, who died in 1989, was a survivor of the sinking of the *Lancastria*. She told me the heart-rending story of what he went through on that fateful day and how it affected him and his family for the rest of their lives.

Before the war he had worked as a platelayer on the railways and after enlisting in the Army on 22 November 1939, he was posted to serve with the Royal Engineers, where he became Sapper 1899060 John Glackin with the 159th Railway Construction Company. His Army service record shows that he arrived in France as part of the British Expeditionary Force on 29 March 1940 and that he returned to England on 18 June 1940, the day after the *Lancastria* was sunk, but there is no mention of the fact that he had been one of those on board the vessel at the time it was lost. Nor is there any mention of the fact that he was then admitted to hospital. It is as if it never happened.

John continued serving with his unit for the rest of the war and was finally demobbed on 15 December 1945, when he was placed on the Army Reserve, Class 'Z', which meant that he could be recalled if it was deemed necessary to do so, but only up until he was 45 years of age.

This is how Bernadette Glackin told me her story:

My dad was one of those who survived the sinking of the *Lancastria*, but what he went through that day, scarred him for the rest of his life. He never did get over it.

When I was a child, I remember him talking about the war, the Germans and the sinking of the *Lancastria*. Looking back all those years ago, I wish I had taken more interest and asked him more questions but as I said, I was only a child of about 11 and the war was not something that I knew too much about or was really that interested in, to be honest. Now, all these years later as I look back, I wish I had asked him more about it, but I didn't. The war wasn't really something that my father could handle talking about it. He became quite emotional when he did.

One night he started talking about the sinking of the *Lancastria*. I will always remember his words; they will stay with me forever. His exact words were, *'we were packed in like sardines in a can, army, navy, air force, civilians, men, women and children, as many as 8,000, maybe even more than that.'* They had just left the harbour at St Nazaire when the German air fighters came in and started to fire upon them, my dad didn't know what had hit them. He made, or tried, to make his way to the top deck of the ship, this alone gave him nightmares day after day, week after week, we all remember this.

When the ship was bombed as it left the harbour, the Jerry aircraft returned and opened fire with their machine guns, shooting at anyone and anyone they could see in the water. One of those was my father. He was terrified. He kept swimming, eventually he had to swim under the water because the ship's leaking fuel was still on fire. He described how he had to move dead fish and other marine life out of the way with his arms as he swam. Eventually he was picked up by a trawler and taken to safety.

I can't remember exactly how long he spent in hospital afterwards, all that sticks in my mind is how it really affected him after the war, every day of his life. He always had tears in his eyes whenever he spoke about the *Lancastria*, especially when he watched the ceremony at the Cenotaph in London every year.

'They'll never talk about it,' he said, *'It's terrible, the people should know what happened back then, how many gave their lives, yet they'll never admit it. Churchill set a D-notice on it, not to be spoke about for one hundred years. It was the biggest maritime disaster of our time, and it has been disregarded like a piece of rubbish,'* he said.

My dad's story after the war is a very poignant one. He went to work as a welder on the railways, for British Rail, or Barney Riley as he like to refer to it as, but my memories of him from when I was a child include him being drunk on a regular basis. Let me explain.

Our mother died, in October 1965, when I was just 10 years of age. It was sad enough that she died, but the fact that she was only 40 at the time, made it even worst. I was one of nine children, six girls and three boys. The eldest was 16 and the youngest was just 14 months old, that's when we heard about the sinking of the *Lancastria*, and my father took to the drink. At the time I, along with my brothers, were disgusted, but now as grown-ups we understand that for a relatively young man of 50 years of age, to lose his wife who was ten years younger than him must have been horrible, and remember there was no help for such matters in those days.

Anyhow, Auld John, as we called him would come in at night with a few drinks in him and that's all he talked about, the war, the Germans and the sinking of the *Lancastria*.

It was clear from talking with Bernadette that she still felt passionately about the sinking of the *Lancastria* and what happened, not just because of her father, but everybody who was on board, both those who survived and those who didn't.

How dare they treat those people like that, even in this day and age the British Government will still not fully recognise what happened? I believe that it is such a shame that the relevant authorities have taken such a stance on the matter. At least the Scottish Government decided to recognise it and went as far as awarding medals to all survivors, known victims, or the relatives of both of those categories. My sister Norah applied for our father's medal, which she subsequently received on his behalf, and has since passed it on to her son, Charles.

Another thing, which initially I forgot to mention, is when the *Lancastria* was bombed, my dad said that when they were jumping ship, on board they were cutting the lifeboats free which then fell on the heads of people who were already in the water. He said he could hear the sounds of their skulls being crushed like coconuts.

Bernadette went on to describe how the family managed after their mother died:

My sister Margaret, was the oldest at that time, just 16 years of age. She took to looking after the three youngest members of the family, Phillip, who was 5, Bernard who was 3, and Delia, who was just 14 months. Then everything took a turn. My Auntie, Marie Julie, who was my dad's sister and was a nun in the Convent of Notre Dame, suggested to him that it would be better if the youngest of us, Delia, stayed with his brother Eddie, who also worked on the railway as a train driver, and his wife Mary, just until she was of school age. That didn't happen, instead my auntie and uncle adopted Delia, but she grew up knowing she was adopted and had two dads. I went with them the night they took her to my aunts, I was heartbroken, it was really sad.

Then my mother's brother, uncle Hugh McNally, started looking after my brother Bernard, but he became really unsettled, and it was then my dad said, 'enough is enough, there's no more of you going anywhere, you're all staying put.' This showed that despite our dad's suffering at the loss of our mother, and the memories and nightmares that he had to deal with because of the sinking of the Lancastria, he was still strong enough to look after his family at what was such a difficult time for us all.

My Auntie Marie Julie was our Guardian Angel. She would bring food from the convent to feed us all, God bless her. To be honest if it wasn't for her, we don't know where we would be today. She is dead now, but it was largely down to her that our family was able to stay together. We had nothing, but we all stuck together through thick and thin, and we would never let anyone say a bad word about our father.

A truly remarkable story about a survivor of the *Lancastria* and his family.

CHAPTER 10

Those Who Died

Those who were lost when the *Lancastria* was sunk were from numerous different regiments and corps. I have recorded their names across the following pages of this chapter, separated into their individual units and in alphabetical order. I have done this by checking the Commonwealth War Graves Commission website and looking at all individuals who are recorded as having been killed or died of their wounds on 17 June 1940. I was able to disregard any member of the Royal Navy who died on that date, because as far as I know, nobody from the Royal Navy was on board the *Lancastria* when she was sunk.

If I have missed anybody through an oversight, then I apologise, but the possibility of such an oversight is added to because of the uncertainty of exactly how many people were lost with the sinking of the ship. To the best of my knowledge I have captured the names of every British serviceman who was known to have died when the *Lancastria* was bombed and sunk.

The men listed below are those recorded on the Commonwealth War Graves Commission website, as having lost their lives whilst serving in France on 17 June

1940, some of the entries even record the words, *'Lost on SS Lancastria'*.

Argyll & Sutherland Highlanders

Sergeant 2976833 John **Blain**
Private 2982611 Robert **Brand**
Private 4341767 John **Caulfield**
Private 2984114 Richard **Cooper**
Private 2974230 Roland **Nock**
Private 2974231 Robert **Smith**

Army Educational Corps

Sergeant 7720882 Henry Austin **Harker**

Bedfordshire and Hertfordshire Regiment

Private 5945648 Albert Charles **Anderson**
Company Quarter Master Sergeant 7143482 Patrick **Manley**

The Buffs (Royal East Kent Regiment)

Private 6288403 Raymond Harold **Batt**
Private 6288801 Alfred Isaac **Baum**
Private 6466737 George William **Brown**
Private 6466508 Frank Desmond **Bull**
Private 6288041 George Thomas **Button**
Private 6289218 Henry **Coomber**
Private 6286543 Gerald **Flowers**
Private 6466563 Leslie **Freeman**
Private 6466566 Alfred Arthur **Gardiner**
Private 6289187 Phillip William **Greenfield**
Private 6466573 Geoffrey Frank **Gregory**
Private 6284468 Thomas Henry **Hatton**
Private 6289138 Eric Philip **Hesleden**

Lance Corporal 6286979 Percy Cecil **Horne**
Private 6289166 Dennis Arthur **Lyrick**
Private 6289068 Ronald **Macdonald-Malekin**
Private 6285455 James **Maloney**
Private 6286788 Ernest Edwin **Payne**
Private 6289212 Norman James **Prosser**
Private 6289036 Ernest Albert **Rogers**
Private 6285362 James Alec **Sellen**
Private 6289225 Charles Kenneth **Smith**
Private 6289230 Philip Sidney **Wardle**
Private 6289267 Jack **Watts**
Private 6289193 William George **Williams**
Private 6287876 Robert **Wright**

Cheshire Regiment

Colour Sergeant 4119665 Harry Lawrence **Hibbins**
Private 4189138 Horace **James**
Private 4188090 Arthur **Keenan**
Private 4188602 Albert **Lewis**
Lance Corporal 4122024 David **Smith**
Private 4186887 Isaac Frederick **Woodland**
Private 4121385 Alfred **Wright**

Devonshire Regiment

Private 5612030 William George **Perry**

Duke of Wellington (West Riding Regiment)

Private 4612249 William **Galloway**

Durham Light Infantry

Private 6395257 Frederick George **Armstrong**
Private 4459151 Edward Terry **Fishwick**

Essex Regiment

Private 5822542 Ernest George **Gibbs**
Private 6009238 Maurice **Gowers**

East Surrey Regiment

Private 6448515 Herbert Henry **Clarke**
Private 6768903 Frederick **Long**
Private 6136583 Reuben **Snell**
Private 5243496 William Henry **Van**
Lance Corporal 6083113 John Matthew **Wild**

East Yorkshire Regiment (The Duke of York's Own)

Colour Sergeant 4342155 William **Morris** (Attached to the
    Auxiliary Military Pioneer Corps)

Gordon Highlanders

Private 811676 Peter Elder **Wedderburn**

Hampshire Regiment

Private 2694234 Allan Roland John **Cobb**

King's Own Scottish Borderers

Private 3183638 Richard Stanley **Baty**
Private 318306 William John **Chapman**
Private 3193730 Stanley Victor **Cummings**
Private 3188162 William John **Glendinning**
Private 3193080 Frederick **Reekie**

King's Shropshire Light Infantry

Corporal 4029688 James **Griffiths**
Lance Corporal 4031197 William **Tomlinson**

Lancashire Fusiliers

Sergeant 3440142 George **Newby**

Fusilier 3525214 John **Rudman**

Manchester Regiment

Private 3523903 William **Nelson**

Private 3519468 William **Turner**

Private 3522627 Dennis **Wilkins**

Corps of Royal Military Police

Lance Corporal 7686963 Stanley Joseph **Barclay**

Lance Corporal 7687025 Hamish Addis **Black**

Lance Corporal 796474 Donald **Theobald**

North Staffordshire Regiment (The Prince of Wales's)

Private 5045351 Jeffrey **Cook**

Corporal 5044351 Albert **Fletcher**

Private 4800138 Henry John **Holsworth**

Private 5046758 Albert Denis **Kelly**

Private 5044717 William Arthur **Mayer**

Corporal 5043943 William H **Meddings**

Private 5046962 William Thomas **Milton**

Private 5046778 Thomas **Roberts**

Private 5044148 James Charles **Rozier**

Lance Corporal 5044759 Walter **Shelbourne**

Private 5047269 Samuel **Smith**

Private 5044881 George **Sutton**

Private 5044931 Harry **Walker**

Private 5044408 Joshua William Albert **Warren**

Private 4911729 James Henry **Williams**

Private 2215645 James **Wright**

Queen's Own Cameron Highlanders

Warrant Officer Class II 2923773 David **Watson**

Queen's Own (Royal West Kent Regiment)

Private 6198727 Edward George **Elms**
Private 6200532 Sidney Herbert **Everett**
Private 6198942 Jeremiah **Galvin**
Private 6196256 Arthur George **Gigg**
Lance Corporal 6199269 William Charles **Sheen**
Private 6336894 Joseph Henry **Watson**

Queen's Own Royal Regiment (West Surrey)

Corporal 772805 Samuel William **Dubery** (Att'd Pioneer
    Corps)
Private 6093154 John Philip **Luff**

Royal Berkshire Regiment

Private 5333700 Walter Henry **Tanner**

Royal Fusiliers (City of London Regiment)

Fusilier 6457466 Arthur **Stevens**
Fusilier 6457504 Frederick **Kendall**
Captain 46277 Herbert John **Webster**

Royal Corps of Signals

Signalman 2587164 Harry **Bennett**
Signalman 2587538 James Alfred **Drabble**
Signalman 2587086 Eric **Dyer**
Signalman 2587556 Clifford **Holland**
Signalman 2587568 John **Jones**
Signalman 2587688 Ernest **McGowan**

Royal Artillery

Gunner 1426292 Leonard Walter **Able**

Gunner 1519234 Herbert **Barrett**

Gunner 831673 John George **Beckwith**

Gunner 1490629 Dennis George **Beeson**

Gunner 1073264 James **Belshaw**

Gunner 1518173 William Ernest **Brown**

Sergeant 1417330 James William Arthur **Burke**

Gunner 1490673 John **Burrows**

Gunner 881931 Albert Norman Winston **Champley**

Gunner 879727 Ernest Charles **Chapman**

Gunner 2566837 Gordon Henry **Chapman**

Gunner 1528702 Peter **Connor**

Gunner 2037797 Guy Allen **Crow**

Gunner 835333 Edwin Stanley **Davis**

Gunner 5568314 Walter George **Davis**

Gunner 3703664 George Iley **Dixon**

Gunner 1428756 Kenneth Douglas **Finnie**

Lance Bombardier 819180 Peter Paul **Finnigan**

Gunner 1554266 Alfred James **Fleming**

Lt-Colonel 49732 Thomas James **Groves**

Gunner 1490842 Ronald Edward **Hickman**

Gunner 786739 Thomas Henry **Hughes**

Gunner 1512207 Cyril **Hunt**

Gunner 1490859 George **Hunter**

Gunner 824105 William Henry **Jenkins**

Gunner 1451993 Sidney Joseph **Kinch**

Gunner 788435 Gerard **McKeown**

Gunner 1491015 Sidney **Rayner**

Gunner 1491042 Bernard George **Rudd**

Gunner 1491047 Joseph William **Sales**

Gunner 1491050 John Charles **Sapsford**
Gunner 1491085 John Frederick **Spooner**
Gunner 1465636 James **Thompson**
Gunner 1491110 Henry Edgar **Tindall**
Gunner 2036531 Edward Arthur **Turnbull**
Gunner 6538895 Herbert Francis **Underhill**
Gunner 871153 Sidney **Waine**
Gunner 1452462 Graham John **West**
Gunner 1446244 Clifford **Wilkinson**

Royal Armoured Corps

Trooper 3644831 Albert **Braddock**
Trooper 4267313 Charles **Carver**
Trooper 7901391 Roy **Clark**
Trooper 409508 Alfred Eric **Collins**
Sergeant 6600 Thomas George **Diamond**
Trooper 318806 Eric Arthur Clifford **Dudman**
Trooper 310772 Thomas William **Edgeworth**
Trooper 420063 Daniel **Graham**
Trooper 7899967 Douglas Edward **Herring**
Trooper 7897002 Cecil William Joseph **Hill**
Warrant Officer Class II Oliver **Hingle**
Trooper 558044 Fred **Hulme**
Trooper 7903384 Edward Charles **Hurst**
Trooper 7902192 Robert Leslie **Jinks**
Trooper 7890659 William **Kidd**
Corporal 5184346 Ronald **Lewis**
Sergeant 398311 Percy Samuel **Orgee**
Trooper 7896959 Arthur Mervyn **Pullin**
Trooper 7905391 George Edward **Reese**
Trooper 421137 Austin Easton **Richardson**
Trooper 7901263 Eric Mons **Sanders**

Warrant Officer Class II Ernest James **Savin**
Corporal 6142199 George Andrew **Skeen**
Corporal 310811 Thomas Ralph **Sturgess**
Trooper 7899228 Francis Oliver **Walkden**
Trooper 7902156 Frederick **Wood**
Trooper 551922 Albert Edward **Wort**

Royal Army Medical Corps

Private 7536057 William Henry **Attwood**
Private 5769299 Reginald John **Elvin**
Private 315951 John **Haselton**
Private 7260657 Neil Grant **Hunter**
Private 7264851 Jack **Lappin**
Private 7263312 James Francis **McNally**
Lieutenant 127123 Anthony James **Moon**
Private 7263977 Raymond Edward **Wells**

Royal Army Pay Corps

Lance Sergeant 7658670 William Horace **Byne**
Lance Sergeant 5172653 Frederick Thomas C. **Cannon**
Private 7663275 Alexander Johnston **Clacher**
Corporal 7658735 Cecil **Cox**
Sergeant 7658221 Reginald Leonard **Dorkins**
Private 7663192 Samuel **Dunphie**
Corporal 7258100 Cyril George **Dunstall**
Sergeant 7811580 Charles William **Franks**
Private 7663694 Gerald Hubert **Golby**
Private 7661757 John Lessels **Gordon**
Private 7667695 Roy **Griggs**
Private 7662918 Robert **Hemingway**
Staff Sergeant 7658213 Charles Bowyer **Lowe**
Private 7663824 George James **Morgan**

Private 7662453 Eric Roy **Paterson**
Sergeant 386297 George Chesterfield **Raper**
Private 7662375 Eric Hudson **Smith**
Private 7662418 John **Smith**
Private 7663512 David William **Spriddle**
Private 106147 James Harold **Thomas**
Private 5998256 Frederick George **Treves**
Private 7667979 Richard Ernest **Trevethan**
Private 74731 Francis Herbert **Wilson**
Private 7659901 Jack George **Winer**

Royal Northumberland Fusiliers

Fusilier 4267095 Joseph Desmond **O'Connor**
Fusilier 4271946 Benjamin **Thomas**

Royal Ulster Rifles

Rifleman 7009511 Alexander **Wright**

Royal Welch Fusiliers

Fusilier 4195636 Joseph Idris **Rowlands**
Fusilier 4195662 Stanley Francis **Shuker**
Fusilier 4195077 George Ivor Maurice **Williams** (Att'd
   Pioneer Corps)

Sherwood Foresters (Notts & Derby Regiment)

Private 4976666 Frank **Beck**
Private 4978940 Albert Sephton **Bennett**
Sergeant 4971155 John Charles **Boardman**
Private 4975922 Reuben **Braisby**
Private 4978391 Francis Ernest Raynor **Brown**
Private 4978811 Sidney **Brown**
Private 4978980 Sydney **Cowlishaw**

Private 4978948 Jack **Doughty**

Corporal 4968706 Thomas **Goodwin**

Private 4978379 Charles **Griffiths**

Private 4977771 Gordon **Holroyd**

Private 4977724 Edward Henry **Holt**

Lance Corporal 4976196 Harold **Hopewell**

Private 4976758 Harold Edward **Johnson**

Private 4975967 John William **Johnson**

Sergeant 4970786 Thomas Taylor **Johnson**

Private 4968691 Timothy **Kerry**

Private 4978210 Arthur Fairbrother **Kitching**

Private 4978633 Clarence Eric **Martin**

Warrant Officer Class II Walter Samuel **McPhun**

Private 4978228 Walter **Newbitt**

Private 4978347 John **O'Loughlin**

Private 4975823 Samuel Henry **Parry**

Private 4743839 Harry **Quarmby**

Private 4978856 Joseph Lambley **Saxton**

Private 4976867 Thomas **Saxton**

Private 4978638 David George **Sherratt**

Private 4978595 Ernest **Smedley**

Sergeant 4974626 Charles **Smith**

Private 4971600 George Edward **Smith**

Private 4977532 Harold **Smith**

Private 4977731 Jack **Storer**

Private 4978640 Leslie **Tacey**

Private 4978266 John Henry **Taylor**

Private 4978944 Arthur **Teagle**

Private 4975703 Thomas Dennis **Voce**

Private 4978725 George Bowmer **Weekley**

Private 4977756 John Stanley **Williams**

Private 4978795 Douglas **Woodward**

South Lancashire Regiment

Private 36544799 Arthur Austin **Place**

South Staffordshire Regiment

Lance Corporal 4910570 Horace **Allen**
Lance Corporal 4911894 Reuben **Cheetham**
Private 4912693 Lionel William **Clements**
Private 4913025 Stanley **Griffiths**
Private 4910583 Samuel **Hepworth**
Lance Corporal 4911193 Thomas Allen **Hutchinson**
Private 4911487 John Henry **Johnson**
Private 4911306 Edmund **Lowe**
Private 4911522 Alfred **Miller**
Private 4909129 John Thomas **Nolan**
Private 4909129 John **Thomas**
Private 4910105 Frederick Charles **Wilson**

South Wales Borderers

Corporal 4073087 Francis James **Birch**
Private 3907155 Edward **Owen**

York and Lancaster Regiment

Private 4742642 John Alan **Airey**
Private 4742538 Ernest **Bower**
Private 4741128 Ernest Robert **Davis**
Lance Corporal 4741171 John Frederick **Delaney**
Private 4741358 Frank **Marsden**
Lance Corporal 4744499 Thomas **McGary**
Private 4744654 James **Ridge**
Private 4745010 George Arthur **Russell**
Private 4742171 Edward **Sykes**

Private 4744281 Leonard **Thomas**
Private 4747156 John **White**
Private 4743120 Richard **Woodhouse**

Merchant Navy (Crew of SS *Lancastria*)

Steward Thomas A **Adams**
Steward Thomas **Amos**
Steward James **Austin**
Sailor William Peter **Ball**
Sailor Michael **Boyle**
Section Man Herbert **Bradley**
Chief Steward Norman Lord **Briscoe**
Bar Keeper Thomas Lonsdale **Clarke**
Section Man Joseph **Coffey**
Assistant Steward William J **Coman**
Sailor Albert Michael **Connor**
Trimmer Ernest James **Croft**
Assistant Steward Albert **Cunningham**
Deck Boy John Frederick **Darley**
Greaser Thomas **Devlin**
Porter Robert **Dingle**
Steward Edward Douglas **Duck**
Senior 2nd Engineer Officer James **Duncan**
Waiter Herbert Richard **Dunmore**
Steward John **Eades**
Chief Master at Arms Alexander Irvine **Fraser**
Steward Thomas Henry **Frodsham**
Steward Henry **Gilbert**
Assistant Cook Joseph **Green**
Able Seaman Arthur Lawson **Hawes**
Boatswain William **Hayden**

Assistant Steward James **Haynes**
Surgeon John **Hill**
Waiter James **Hughes**
Waiter Harry A **Illidge**
Seaman Jacob Cowie **Imlach**
Steward Harry **Jackson**
Captain's Steward Stanley Louis Frederic **Key**
Greaser Robert George **Major**
Assistant Bar Keeper Joseph **Marshallsay**
Trimmer John **Mason**
Storekeeper Samuel Alexander **McCaw**
Tourist Bath Steward John **McDonald**
Cook Owen **McGorrin**
Assistant Cook Walter **Mottershead**
Steward Thomas John **Oliver**
Assistant Baker Frederick **Owen**
Boatswain William Henry **Parsons**
Chef Joseph **Pearse**
Junior Assistant Purser Cuthbert Edgar **Porter**
Chief Butcher Thomas Douglas **Read**
First Officer Richard Goronwy **Roberts**
Steward Herbert **Rogers**
Steward Arthur **Rogerson**
Porter Thomas **Rowe**
Third Officer Reginald Gordon **Rumney**
Waiter Edward John **Ryan**
Dispenser Fred **Shepherd**
Steward William H **Slater**
Steward Joseph Edwin **Smith**
Steward Wilfred George **Smith**
Steward John Herbert **Snowdon**
Assistant Steward Patrick **Stanton**

Ordinary Seaman Robert **Surtees**
Steward Thomas **Taylor**
Porter Edgar **Temby**
Able Seaman George Henry **Tilston**
Fireman Patrick J **Walsh**
Trimmer Joseph **Walton**

Pioneer Corps

Private 13005223 Albert Edward **Allinson**
Sergeant 4737269 Joseph **Andrews**
Private 5242384 Robert John **Andrews**
Sergeant 7606674 Patrick **Anthony**
Private 13005225 Augustus **Apetu-Larty**
Private 13002461 Clifford William **Arey**
Private 13003423 Walter Herbert **Armstrong**
Lance Corporal 3381296 James **Ashworth**
Private 13007657 Royal **Ashworth**
Private 2185475 Norman Ernest **Astle**
Private 13005631 Albert **Attwood**
Lance Corporal 13009499 Frederick **Attwood**
Private 13001811 Arthur George **Avis**
Private 2188527 Benjamin **Axcell**
Private 13005211 George William **Aynsley**
Private 13007283 Robert **Ayre**
Private 1446738 Joseph **Baker**
Private 13001467 Charles **Baldwin**
Sergeant 754746 Thomas **Baldwin**
Private 2188568 Arthur **Ball**
Private 2022442 Harold Collins **Ballam**
Private 3701642 Arthur Edward **Barnaby**
Private 7607102 Peter **Barnes**
Private 13002420 George **Barnsley**

Private 13006023 Ernest **Barr**
Private 13006077 John **Barry**
Private 13002841 Frederick John **Batten**
Private 2188534 Albert **Baugh**
Private 2188368 Alfred **Beaumont**
Private 13001392 Frank **Beaver**
Private 13005168 Percy **Beaver**
Private 3902029 Arthur Joseph **Bedell**
Private 2188369 Frank William **Bendall**
Private 2191159 David William **Bennett**
Private 2181172 George Thompson **Bickerstaff**
Private 13003785 Thomas **Bidgood**
Private 101269 Ronald **Bingham**
Private 13000444 William Robert **Bishop**
Private 2185508 Norman **Booth**
Private 13005833 George Thomas **Bourn**
Private 2188943 Joseph **Boyle**
Private 13001137 Albert John **Bradford**
Private 13005273 Edward **Brady**
Private 13003391 John **Brady**
Corporal 1300638 George **Braidwood**
Corporal 13000857 Francis Henry John **Brain**
Private 13005244 Victor Sidney **Brampton**
Private 2188500 Frederick William **Bridle**
Private 1452391 Joseph **Briggs**
Private 13004948 Stanley **Brook**
Private 13001398 Robert **Broomhead**
Lance Corporal 6909735 Thomas Henry **Brown**
Private 13000452 William **Brown**
Private 2188374 Joseph William **Bryans**
Private 13001139 Robert Edward John **Bryant**
Private 2181327 Victor George **Buckingham**

Private 13004946 Samuel **Budby**
Private 13003050 Thomas **Burke**
Private 13004622 Owen **Burns**
Corporal 529164 William **Burns**
Private 13005334 Leonard **Burton**
Private 13000535 Ernest Alfred **Busby**
Corporal 13003637 Charles Henry **Butcher**
Private 2182540 Thomas Taylor **Butterworth**
Private 13005313 Walter **Butterworth**
Corporal 13005058 Harold **Bytheway**
Private 7253152 Davis **Caborn**
Corporal 2188410 George **Cadbury**
Private 4441270 John Andrew **Cain**
Private 13001818 Archibald **Carchrie**
Private 5104872 Francis Henry **Carless**
Lance Corporal 13005181 Thomas **Carr**
Private 7606823 William **Carr**
Lance Corporal 13005016 William Robson **Carr**
Private 13005496 Thomas **Carroll**
Private 7615198 James Patrick **Casey**
Private 13006840 Herbert Edward **Catlin**
Corporal 6972225 James **Cavanagh**
Private 103245 Reuben Holly **Channing**
Private 13005966 Henry John **Chapman**
Private 13005382 John Edward **Charlotte**
Private 3590558 John James **Chowns**
Private 13001209 George John **Clark**
Private 13005747 Herbert **Clark**
Private 13001820 John **Clark**
Private 13002051 George **Clarke**
Private 13002477 Edward **Clarkson**
Private 13002053 Harry **Cliffe**

Private 6284318 John William George **Cloake**
Private 2183857 John **Clyne**
Private 13001950 Edward **Cochrane**
Private 13004219 George **Cocklin**
Private 13001140 Louis **Cogger**
Private 13001404 George **Collins**
Private 102591 William **Conn-Hall**
Private 2188397 Daniel **Cooper**
Private 2184102 Walter Alan **Cooper**
Corporal 1001001 Arthur **Cope**
Private 13004995 Leonard **Copley**
Private 13005433 Charles **Cox**
Private 2183072 Charles **Cox**
Private 13003568 William **Crawford**
Private 13001821 Walter **Croft**
Corporal 2185400 James Joseph **Cummings**
Sergeant 4850010 William Edward **Cunliffe**
Private 13006008 James Dennis **Cunningham**
Private 13002300 Thomas **Cusick**
Private 13001451 George William **Dale**
Private 2188548 Thomas Edward **Daniel**
Private 13005230 Bert **Davies**
Private 2191495 Ernest Edward **Davies**
Private 1043424 John William **Davison**
Private 2188360 Frederick **Deards**
Private 13000110 Robert **Delaney**
Private 102344 James **Dennison**
Corporal 2188599 Joe **Derbyshire**
Corporal 2186767 William Henry **Dewis**
Private 13001478 Thomas John **Dicks**
Private 13001945 Andrew **Doherty**
Private 2188394 David Forbes **Donald**

Private 2181356 Albert Ernest **Downey**
Private 2188975 Edward Arthur **Downs**
Corporal 102338 Martin **Doyle**
Lance Corporal 5875691 Daniel **Driscoll**
Private 2191368 David Alexander **Duncan**
Private 13001409 Walter **Duncan**
Private 13002839 John **Dunn**
Private 13005355 Albert **Dunnington**
Private 2184038 Thomas **Earle**
Corporal 5042446 James **Easom**
Private 1023063 Walter Henry **Easterbrook**
Private 7613264 Harry **Eden**
Private 5249871 John **Edge**
Private 13005275 Thomas Henry **Edmondson**
Private 5878067 Alfred Andrew **Elliott**
Private 4337743 John James **Elsdon**
Private 13003422 Leonard **Elvin**
Private 13003804 Edward **Embury**
Corporal 5718466 Lionel **England**
Private 1012280 William **Escreet**
Private 13002056 John **Evans**
Private 2184039 Walter Cyril **Evans**
Private 5104434 Harry **Eyles**
Private 13002427 John **Fairhurst**
Private 2182004 Edward **Farrar**
Private 13006680 George **Farrar**
Private 2188411 Albert **Farrer**
Private 15957 James **Ferrie**
Private 13002474 Thomas **Fetigan**
Private 2185530 Albert Alfred **Fichou**
Private 4380141 William **Finlay**
Private 13004019 Harry **Firkins**

Private 2188449 John **Flaherty**
Private 4691095 Albert **Fone**
Private 7606888 Robert **Forde**
Private 13005497 James **Forrester**
Private 2189224 John **Forsyth**
Private 13005214 George Henry **Foulds**
Private 13005091 George **Fowler**
Sergeant 2186362 Richard **Fowler**
Private 13005898 Gilbert **Frudd**
Private 13005546 John **Gallagher**
Private 102376 Thomas **Gannon**
Private 1021278 William **Garside**
Corporal 13002431 George **Gaskell**
Private 2188462 Thomas **Gawith**
Private 13003554 Douglas Laing **Geekie**
Private 2188300 Samuel **Gellatly**
Private 21885909 Charles **Gibson**
Private 13004998 Robert Henry **Gibson**
Private 13006666 James **Gill**
Private 13005262 Walter **Gillies**
Private 13004210 James Frank **Godfrey**
Private 3123462 Peter **Goldie**
Private 4529713 Michael **Gorman**
Corporal 2188590 Joseph Francis **Gorringe**
Private 4440783 Thomas George **Graham**
Private 2184064 Alphonso Kinmont **Grant**
Private 13006032 William Albert **Green**
Private 3847072 Fred **Greenwood**
Private 13001829 William **Green**
Private 13005465 George Oswald **Gregg**
Private 13002783 Walter **Greig**
Corporal 392162 Alfred Rees **Griffiths**

Private 13011221 George **Griffiths**
Private 4026258 John Edward **Griffiths**
Corporal 2306160 Alfred Arthur **Grimmett**
Private 2188513 George **Hadley**
Private 2188407 Edwin **Hall**
Private 13002274 Horace **Hall**
Corporal 4445254 John William **Hall**
Private 13003373 Samuel **Hall**
Private 2182526 Lewis William **Hancock**
Private 13001316 Martin **Hanley**
Private 13004621 Ernest Victor **Hare**
Private 13005503 John Thomas **Harris**
Private 4535726 Edward **Harrison**
Lance Corporal 13005010 Frederick Georges **Harrison**
Private 2188423 Ronald James **Harrison**
Private 2188455 Thomas **Harrison**
Private 2181707 William Henry **Harrison**
Private 13005648 William **Harrop**
Private 101096 Walter **Hartley**
Private 13002457 William **Hayes**
Private 13005001 Frederick William **Heath**
Private 2183365 John James **Heggety**
Private 13005340 William **Hewitt**
Private 3856961 Clifford Gordon **Heywood**
Private 2188669 Hubert Thomas **Hickerton**
Private 6908838 Horace **Hicks**
Private 3123314 Arthur Thomas **Highley**
Private 13002606 Horace **Hinks**
Private 13006799 William George Richard **Hissey**
Private 13005931 James Patrick **Hoban**
Private 101368 Gideon **Hope**
Private 102896 Edwin Walter **Hopgood**

Private 2185416 Stephen Anthony **Horan**
Sergeant 218006 Thomas **Hordern**
Private 13001247 Thomas Edward **Houghton**
Private 13004957 Eric **Howard**
Lance Corporal 490628 Frederick **Howard**
Corporal 2188456 John **Hulme**
Private 4793945 William **Hutchinson**
Private 2188321 Harold **Ingham**
Private 13002886 Kenneth Sydney **Ings**
Private 2188312 John Edward **Ireland**
Private 13003839 John **Irvine**
Private 315521 James Brewer **Isaac**
Corporal 13005617 Albert Edward **Jackson**
Private 13005099 Frederick **Jackson**
Private 13005372 Stanley **Jackson**
Private 13002605 Henry Augustus **James**
Private 3956763 David **Jarvis**
Private 13005279 John William **Jessop**
Private 102164 Robert Edward **Johnson**
Private 13001000 James **Jones**
Private 7605729 James Lloyd **Jones**
Corporal 1061600 Henry William **Jordon**
Private 219035 Joseph **Judson**
Private 13003852 Phillip **Kearney**
Private 2188572 Daniel **Kelly**
Private 13000243 Frank Matthew **Kelly**
Private 13001552 James **Kelly**
Private 7615077 Owen **Kelly**
Private 7613263 William **Kelly**
Private 2188951 Victor **Kemp**
Private 2184605 Harry **Kennedy**
Private 13005264 Robert Brown **Kennedy**

Private 130005102 Harold **Kershaw**

Lance Corporal 3237769 Edward **Kesson**

Corporal 13000584 Peter **Khan**

Private 2186598 Michael **Killeen**

Private 2188501 Ronald Ernest Harold **King**

Private 4380742 George Frederick **Knowles**

Corporal 2867468 William Robert **Laing**

Private 3233186 Peter **Langford**

Private 2188295 Tony Lawrance **Laquanello**

Private 13002251 John William **Lardant**

Private 13004963 Albert Ernest **Latham**

Private 130002453 Joseph **Law**

Lance Corporal 2183077 John Thomas **Lawley**

Private 1009693 William **Lawrence**

Private 7613262 Leonard **Lea**

Private 13005027 John **Leahy**

Private 13005233 Charles **Leckenby**

Private 13002332 Richard Henry **Lees**

Private 13001292 William **Leighton**

Private 6195176 Leonard George **Leslie**

Company Quartermaster Sergeant John Thomas **Lester**

Private 13002060 David Thomas **Lewis**

Private 2188551 John Henry **Ling**

Private 13005217 Edgar **Liversidge**

Private 13002604 Victor Charles **Loff**

Private 2188640 John **Logan**

Private 3635841 Walter **Long**

Private 13005469 Thomas Frederick **Love**

Lance Corporal 13005051 Charles **Lowther**

Private 13011021 William **Macphee**

Private 2190054 James **Malam**

Private 218446 John **Manning**

Corporal 13000265 Charles Frederick **Marchant**
Lieutenant 43239 Reginald John **Markey**
Private 13002341 William Roberts **Marle**
Private13002733 William **Marsh**
Private 13001642 Benjamin **Marshall**
Private 2188308 Daniel **Martin**
Private 2188547 Frank **Massey**
Private 13006456 Frank **Mather**
Private 7607008 Charles **Matthews**
Private 830282 Joseph Henry **Matthews**
Private 2182395 Philip **Matthews**
Private 7606821 Edward Frederick **Mayers**
Private 2187370 James **McBride**
Private 2182015 Thomas **McCamley**
Private 3635841 James Porter **McColl**
Private 2188553 William **McCormick**
Private 2183234 William **McCue**
Corporal 13006692 John **McDonald**
Private 2182010 William **McDonald**
Private 870263 William Henry James **McDonald**
Private 2183261 John Joseph **McDonough**
Private 2744825 Harry **McDougal**
Private 13005420 William James **McFeggan**
Private 2188489 Henry James Smith **McGuire**
Lance Corporal 2187273 James **McHale**
Private 13001124 Joseph **McKigney**
Corporal 13000284 Patrick **McMahon**
Private 2188934 John **McNamara**
Private 13005220 Joseph **McQuade**
Private 7006739 Daniel **McVeigh**
Private 2189220 James **Melville**
Private 3179660 George Alfred **Melvin**

Private 13005734 John Graham **Mendham**
Private 13003767 Ninion **Metcalfe**
Private 13001931 George **Milburn**
Private 2188361 Terrance George **Miller**
Private 13003869 George **Mills**
Private 2870283 Hudson Taylor **Mitchell**
Lance Corporal 101154 Thomas **Monaghan**
Corporal 2188497 Philip John **Monk**
Private 392826 Joseph James **Moore**
Corporal 13002064 Thomas **Moorhead**
Private 3513210 Roger **Morgan**
Private 7607121 Sydney **Morgan**
Private 13003454 Thomas **Morgan**
Private 2188586 William **Morgan**
Sergeant 4535382 Stanley **Morphet**
Private 2186160 James **Morris**
Private 13003876 John Joseph **Murphy**
Private 7615087 Patrick Joseph **Murphy**
Warrant Officer Class ll John Forbes **Murray**
Lance Corporal 7341103 Walter **Murray**
Private 13005470 Alfred Edward **Myers**
Private 13005344 John Walter **Naylor**
Private 13002780 James **Neave**
Private 2188754 Robert Henry **Neil**
Private 13007917 William **Nelson**
Private 13001431 James **Newton**
Private 13005508 William **Nixon**
Private 13003649 Brinley Charles **Norman**
Private 13000801 Sidney James **Nunn**
Private 2182016 William Frederick **Oakley**
Private 2188517 Alfred **Oare**
Private 2182529 Simon **O'Connell**

Private 13001505 Michael **O'Dowd**

Private 2182543 John **O'Hara**

Private 2182011 Frank **O'Neil**

Private 13004153 William **O'Neil**

Private 4848875 Thomas Henry **Oram**

Corporal 13004970 Thomas William **Owens**

Private 13000992 Sidney Eric **Palmer**

Corporal 2188570 William **Parkin**

Private 804718 Herbert **Patchett**

Corporal 4381206 Herbert **Pattison**

Corporal 13000976 John Robert **Peacock**

Private 1426643 Arthur **Peel**

Private 5094474 Henry George **Perrin**

Private 13001749 Francis **Pope**

Private 13005198 Joseph Henry **Porter**

Private 13001316 Herbert Victor **Potton**

Private 13001434 Randel **Powell**

Sergeant 13002346 Robert William **Powell**

Private 13001164 Joseph Arthur **Prager**

Private 13000785 Josiah **Preston**

Private 3645404 Arthur Edward **Price**

Private 3301428 James Frederick **Ralley**

Private 410467 Victor Cyril **Randall**

Private 803248 Philip Arthur Whitham **Raper**

Private 5242548 Joseph **Reader**

Private 2188356 Edgar Joseph **Renton**

Lance Corporal 13004944 David Leslie **Renwick**

Private 13004976 Ernest **Reynolds**

Private 2183168 William Joseph **Reynolds**

Private 2188337 Thomas Ronald **Richards**

Private 64682 John **Ridley**

Lance Corporal 2971379 Adam **Ritchie**

Corporal 13001510 Charles Henry **Roberts**
Private 2188967 Adam Cail **Robertson**
Private 13005235 Charles William **Robinson**
Private 13004832 Thomas Henry **Robinson**
Private 101436 Thomas **Rushton**
Lance Corporal 13005076 Leslie Ernest **Sams**
Private 1046579 Arthur **Schofield**
Private 13005477 Charles **Scotney**
Private 13009067 Joseph **Scougall**
Private 7252124 Joshua William **Sharp**
Private 5097497 Arthur James **Shepherd**
Private 396897 William **Shepherd**
Private 2183062 James **Shirley**
Private 2188306 Joseph **Silvester**
Private 13004640 Robert Douglas **Simpson**
Private 613778 Reginald Walter **Skilton**
Private 3848792 Oswald **Slate**
Private 13002468 John **Slater**
Private 2188677 Benjamin **Smith**
Corporal 7813684 George Henry **Smith**
Private 13002752 George Joseph **Smith**
Private 13005236 James **Smith**
Private 13001774 John **Smith**
Private 2196053 Joshua **Smith**
Private 13005428 Robert William **Smith**
Private 3435408 Samuel **Smith**
Private 13001169 Stanley Thomas **Smith**
Private 2188416 Thomas Edward **Smith**
Private 13001169 Stanley Thomas **Smith**
Private 2188507 Henry Ernest **Soden**
Private 13001992 Arthur **Stead**
Private 2878226 Alexander Aitken **Stewart**

Private 13009588 William **Stewart**

Private 2188566 John **Stocks**

Private 2186128 Joseph Benjamin **Stone**

Private 13002766 Nicholas **Storey**

Lieutenant 125435 Douglas Albert **Stuart**

Private 101732 William **Sullivan**

Private 2188473 John **Swalwell**

Private 2188964 William Charles **Swan**

Corporal 103834 Samuel **Sykes**

Private 101483 Wilson **Taggart**

Private 2182350 Wilfred John **Tanner**

Private 13002832 Thomas Thompson Allison **Tate**

Private 3436576 Arnold **Taylor**

Lance Corporal 5103109 Harry **Taylor**

Private 13006099 Harry James **Taylor**

Private 13005257 Isaac Joseph **Taylor**

Private 2188408 Thomas **Taylor**

Private 13000389 William Edward **Thomas**

Sergeant 13002487 Peter **Thomason**

Private 13004983 Joseph **Thompson**

Private 2182447 Leon Owen **Toon**

Private 13002817 George **Traviss**

Private 7605537 Thomas **Tunstall**

Warrant Officer Class ll Arthur **Turpin**

Private 13001447 James Alfred **Tyler**

Private 13003783 James **Tynan**

Private 13002428 Frederick **Unsworth**

Corporal 13001448 David **Verity**

Corporal 13000932 John Arthur **Viall**

Private 13005175 Harry George **Vince**

Private 13005519 Leonard **Walsh**

Private 13001592 Thomas **Walters**

Private 2182533 Harry Richard Joseph **Walton**

Private 7250994 Sidney Cantle **Walton**

Private 13002083 Charles **Ward**

Sergeant 2186859 George Albert **Ward**

Private 13006070 William Henry **Ward**

Private 13000409 George **Watson**

Private 5097986 George Edward **Watson**

Private 13004209 John **Watson**

Private 13005347 Robert **Watson**

Private 2188441 Ernest Anthony **Watt**

Private 443857 Samuel **Webb**

Private 2185190 Joseph George James **Webster**

Private2185188 William Charles **Webster**

Corporal 264229 James **Weir**

Sergeant 13005166 John **Whailing**

Private 13005164 Thomas Edward **White**

Corporal 13002422 Claude **Whitehouse**

Private 6394471 Albert Clarence **Wickham**

Sergeant 6895683 Alec Herbert **Wigley**

Private 13001447 John **Wilkins**

Private 2184404 Sidney Bertram **Williams**

Private 13003443 Thomas William **Williams**

Corporal 13001532 William **Williams**

Private 2188686 William Edward **Williams**

Private 2190162 Frederick John **Williamson**

Private 2188847 Henry **Wilson**

Private 13002815 James **Wilson**

Private 2185187 Thomas S F **Windsor**

Private 2188605 William V **Winstanley**

Corporal 13003439 Arthur Reginald **Wood**

Corporal 65940 Edward Gardiner **Woods**

Private 2182534 James **Worthington**

Private 2188953 James **Yeaman**
Private 2188528 Alexander **Young**
Private 13003461 Henry **Young**
Private 13002854 Thomas **Young**

Royal Air Force (RAF)

Flight Sergeant 370706 Hugh Durbin **Alston**
Aircraftman 2nd Class 630625 William **Appleby**
Sergeant 541488 Walter **Ardern**
Aircraftman 2nd Class 940345 Kenneth William **Ashby**
Corporal 350089 Alfred **Ashley**
Sergeant 581492 Leslie George **Baker**
Aircraftman 1st Class 542802 Joseph Edward C **Bardgett**
Leading Aircraftman 547360 George Wellesley **Barrie**
Leading Aircraftman 510961 George William **Bassam**
Leading Aircraftman 535546 George **Bateman**
Corporal 505311 John Robert **Baxter**
Leading Aircraftman 641894 Edmund **Bell**
Sergeant 522900 Joseph Dixon **Bell**
Corporal 525364 Richard Raymond **Bodden**
Aircraftman 1st Class 624402 Thomas Gervais **Booth**
Aircraftman 1st Class 624815 Arnold **Boumphrey**
Leading Aircraftman 614898 Raymond **Broadbent**
Aircraftman 2nd Class 627081 Douglas **Brown**
Corporal 510279 James **Cartwright**
Flight Sergeant 21476 William Francis **Chard**
Aircraftman 1st Class 508618 Frederick S H **Chave**
Aircraftman 1st Class 625723 James Balfour **Christie**
Aircraftman 1st Class 640028 Donald Basil **Clarke**
Corporal 652931 Horace **Clarke**
Leading Aircraftman 518910 Sydney **Clarke**
Corporal 753581 Norman John **Clifford**

Corporal 542816 Norman **Cocking**
Corporal 543598 Robert **Conkie**
Corporal 532979 Albert Charles **Cook**
Aircraftman 1st Class 633627 James William **Cooper**
Leading Aircraftsman 534033 C E **Cormack-Beatson**
Leading Aircraftman 408226 Lionel James **Crane**
Aircraftman 1st Class 618536 James **Cranston**
Corporal 568835 Henry **Daniel**
Sergeant 509566 Thomas Frederick **Denton**
Leading Aircraftman 509271 Harry Duhamel **Derwin**
Leading Aircraftman 535631 George Macdonald **Diamond**
Aircraftman 1st Class 618876 George Alfred **Dignan**
Leading Aircraftman 551107 Herbert George **Edwards**
Corporal 354733 William George **Eldred**
Aircraftman 1st Class 639435 Harry **Fisher**
Leading Aircraftman 551310 Harry **Fisher**
Aircraftman 1st Class 629004 Thomas **Fitzpatrick**
Aircraftman 1st Class 212009 James Ernest **Fothergill**
Corporal 505130 John **Frost**
Aircraftman 1st Class 637128 Patrick **Gavin**
Leading Aircraftman 623072 Walter **Gleave**
Leading Aircraftman 544145 Dennis William **Glover**
Corporal 509633 Charles Alfred **Golding**
Corporal 511338 Francis Lowson **Gordon**
Aircraftman 2nd Class 636117 Kenneth W **Griffin**
Aircraftman 1st Class 627989 Daniel Myrddin **Griffiths**
Aircraftman 1st Class 505901 Reginald George B **Grove**
Aircraftman 1st Class 569713 George Edward **Groves**
Aircraftman 1st Class 617121 Henry Charles **Gunn**
Leading Aircraftman 624110 Hugh Percy F **Guymer**
Corporal 529271 George Thomas **Hall**
Corporal 561175 Andrew George **Hamilton**

Leading Aircraftman 544667 William **Hardisty**

Aircraftman 1st Class Wilfred **Harpham**

Aircraftman 2nd Class 904276 Frank Henry **Hatherly**

Aircraftman 1st Class 624731 Thomas Alfred **Hayes**

Leading Aircraftman 549266 James Isaac **Hepplewhite**

Aircraftman 1st Class 638025 John **Higgins**

Sergeant 631209 George Gresham Stanley **Hills**

Flying Officer 31444 Robert Colin **Hodgson**

Corporal 612270 Alfred Frederick Gordon **Hoe**

Leading Aircraftman 253638 Reginald Alfred **Holland**

Leading Aircraftman 569469 William S **Honderwood**

Aircraftman 2nd Class John Frederick **Hopkinson**

Aircraftman 1st Class 653766 Victor Hugh **How**

Aircraftman 1st Class 630740 Robert **Howell**

Aircraftman 1st Class 639529 Owen **Humphries**

Leading Aircraftman 357304 James **Hutchison**

Corporal 618392 Leonard Addy **I'Anson**

Leading Aircraftman 521686 Ian **Ingraham**

Leading Aircraftman Robert Samuel **Jary**

Sergeant 536553 Charles Phillips **Jones**

Leading Aircraftman 533484 Douglas Walter **Jones**

Leading Aircraftman 544901 Richard Thompson **Jones**

Corporal 528052 Tegwyn Davies **Jones**

Corporal 347116 Fred **Joy**

Leading Aircraftman 542978 Robert Miller **Kelly**

Aircraftman 1st Class 624350 James Edwin **Kent**

Aircraftman 1st Class 639579 John **Kerr**

Corporal 545496 Robert **Kevan**

Corporal 564874 George Roland **King**

Aircraftman 1st Class 278360 Marcus Miller **Landsdowne**

Leading Aircraftman 571314 Gordon Albert **Latter**

Aircraftman 1st Class 613179 Trevor David Samuel **Lloyd**

Aircraftman 1st Class 631821 Wilfred **Lusty**
Aircraftman 1st Class 629386 Alexander **Macauley**
Leading Aircraftman 642192 William **Macpherson**
Leading Aircraftman 536654 Stephen Joseph **Marron**
Aircraftman 2nd Class 334379 John Henry **Mawson**
Aircraftman 1st Class 613055 Henry George **McLeod**
Corporal 591398 Roy Patrick Walter **McMahon**
Corporal 653337 Alfred William **Moore**
Corporal 508119 Ralph **Moore**
Aircraftman 1st Class 619958 James Dominic **Niall**
Aircraftman 1st Class 616532 John Harry **Norris**
Corporal 526717 Albert **Park**
Corporal 358147 Edward **Petrie**
Aircraftman 1st Class 615972 Eric George **Plumb**
Aircraftman 2nd Class 643721 Thomas **Price**
Aircraftman 1st Class 542863 William **Pugh**
Aircraftman 1st Class 618627 William Edward **Radford**
Aircraftman 1st Class 551305 Dennis Joseph **Ramsey**
Aircraftman 2nd Class 621890 Morrison Wilfred J **Ranson**
Leading Aircraftman 354527 Ernest Edward **Rayner**
Leading Aircraftman 122726 George Arthur T **Record**
Aircraftman 1st Class 644120 Leslie **Redfern**
Aircraftman 2nd Class 642662 Eric Charles **Reeves**
Leading Aircraftman 357083 William **Richardson**
Leading Aircraftman 615860 Robert **Riddell**
Corporal 532889 Geoffrey Arthur **Rigby**
Aircraftman 1st Class 625691 Herbert **Robinson**
Corporal 347547 John Burton **Rodgers**
Aircraftman 1st Class 591650 John **Rogers**
Leading Aircraftman 348238 Andrew Garbutt **Roe**
Corporal 523638 William Charles **Rushton**
Leading Aircraftman 629753 Harry Victor **Sargeant**

Aircraftman 1st Class 547248 Peter Wardlaw **Saunders**

Aircraftman 1st Class 624090 Douglas Jack **Scoins**

Aircraftman 1st Class 628742 Andrew John **Scott-Kiddie**

Aircraftman 1st Class 631548 Clarence Frederick **Slater**

Aircraftman 2nd Class 626102 Frederick Horatio **Smith**

Aircraftman 1st Class 654382 Harold Vincent **Smith**

Sergeant 563390 James Terrance **Smith**

Aircraftman 2nd Class 623477 Sydney **Smith**

Aircraftman 1st Class 612896 Walter Lochrie **Smith**

Aircraftman 1st Class 628225 Nicholas **Smyth**

Aircraftman 1st Class 628640 Dennis **Stones**

Leading Aircraftman 619703 John Reid **Storrar**

Aircraftman 1st Class 628702 Albert Leslie **Symmonds**

Leading Aircraftman 614845 Stanley **Taws**

Leading Aircraftman 356773 Albert John **Taylor**

Leading Aircraftman 516061 James Victor L **Thomas**

Flight Sergeant 590139 Gordon Keable **Tidy**

Aircraftman 2nd Class 573560 Cyril **Timms**

Leading Aircraftman 268892 Lawrence **Traynor**

Aircraftman 1st Class 614428 Edward **Tredgett**

Leading Aircraftman 524140 James Albert **Waite**

Aircraftman 1st Class 570036 Keith Memsforth **Walker**

Leading Aircraftman 625205 Francis William **Watkin**

Aircraftman 1st Class 620691 Albert **Watson**

Corporal 525119 Alfred John **Watts**

Leading Aircraftman 632799 Alfred William **Wayman**

Corporal 591163 James **Whittet**

Leading Aircraftman 530579 John Arkell **Williamson**

Leading Aircraftman 532511 William John **Williamson**

Aircraftman 1st Class 636044 Frederick James **Wilson**

Corporal 591172 Walter **Wilson**

Aircraftman 2nd Class 640245 Kenneth Leslie **Wyatt**

Royal Army Service Corps

Private S/106859 Arthur William **Abbott**

Private S/63242 Robert Norman **Abbott**

Lance Corporal S/98848 William Rhodes **Ainsworth**

Lance Corporal T/104001 Douglas John **Andrewartha**

Private S/98410 Robert Cummings **Anthony**

Sergeant S/3767249 Richard **Arends**

Driver T/121391 Thomas Spencer **Armstrong**

Sergeant S/147853 Frank Stanley **Ash**

Private S/112888 Lawrence **Auty**

Driver 88502 James **Ballard**

Driver T/107695 Alfred Edward **Banks**

Driver 110617 Francis Meredith **Barnes**

Private 148581 William Ernest **Barritt**

Private 94912 Rex Edmund **Barry**

Private 105711 Richard **Bayliss**

Driver T/70507 Norman Wilfred **Benns**

Lance Corporal S/74275 William Edward **Biles**

Driver T/118174 George Alfred **Bodimeade**

Lance Corporal T/64906 Frederick Cecil **Bolton**

Driver T/151358 Frederick George **Boniface**

Private S/105301 George **Bowen**

Corporal S/73417 Alan Devenport **Bramley**

Warrant Officer Class II S/94144 Harry **Brand**

Driver T/16921 Leslie Percy **Bray**

Corporal S/147960 Forster Anderson **Brewis**

Private S/147440 Reginald Charles **Britton**

Corporal S/147757 Francis Joseph **Brookhouse**

Private S/115317 Douglas Arthur **Brown**

Private S/137037 Stanley George **Bryson**

Driver T/136129 Harry **Bullock**

Private S/105077 Brian Lonsdale **Burke**

Corporal 52872 Daniel Augustus **Burke**

Private T/153235 Harold **Burnip**

Private 105985 Arthur James **Cail**

Private S/57251 Walter John **Candlin**

Lance Corporal S/52890 Arthur Edmund **Cameron-Waller**

Private 147499 Reginald Mumford St Clair **Campbell**

Driver T/121336 Donald **Carroll**

Corporal 105576 Robert **Chamberlain**

Corporal 105576 Percy William **Chandler**

Corporal 94132 James **Chilton**

Sergeant S/74207 John **Chipchase**

Driver T/77052 Eric William Herbert **Clarke**

Private S/98553 John Frederick **Clay**

Private S/94318 Robert Charles **Cooke**

Private S/94927 John **Cornish**

Driver T/91432 William **Cort**

Driver T/97760 Cyril George **Coward**

Private S/2812343 Alexander **Cruickshank**

Captain 52451 Reginald Francis Raymond **Currey**

Private S/94749 Robert Frank **Curry**

Sergeant S/5041642 Lawrence **Cyples**

Private S/2034530 William James **Dalgarno**

Corporal 105081 Edward John **Danks**

Private 147923 Charles Rees **Davies**

Private S/97270 Leslie **Davies**

Lance Corporal T/7576367 Richard **Davies**

Private S/162752 Norman **Dawson**

Private T/109261 William Arthur **Day**

Driver T/158277 Frederick Charles **Denison**

Private S/165631 Leslie Gordon **Derham**

Private S/119050 David Theodore **Donald**

Private S/13854 Herbert Kitchener **Douglas**

Private S/133108 Claude Cyril Montgomery **Downes**
Corporal T/94304 Frederick **Doyle**
Lance Corporal S/54234 Leslie George **Duck**
Lance Corporal T/71154 Thomas Nesbet **Dunning**
Corporal 105133 Donald Phillips **Durrant**
Private S/119036 Edward George **Dwyer**
Sergeant T/33717 Leonard William **Dyas**
Corporal 54849 Albert Edward **Dyke**
Driver T/45585 Albert Henry **Edwards**
Private 147926 Douglas Malcolm **Edwards**
Private 147447 Sidney George **Edwards**
Private 99502 James Charles **Ellis**
Private T/43579 Thomas **Etherington**
Private 132843 Albert Edward **Evans**
Private 98705 David Emlyn **Evans**
Private S/73506 John Raymond **Evans**
Private 47931 Charles Thomas **Fahie**
Private S/108399 Arnold Lawrence **Falconbridge**
Private 147431 Donald **Farrell**
Corporal 63904 Richard Frederick Hooper **Findlay**
Private S/98215 Soloman **Fleisher**
Private 105844 Michael Gerard **Fox**
Sergeant 94087 Albert Henry **Garrett**
Private T/63177 Norman **Gibson**
Private T/63358 Arthur George **Gompertz**
Private T/109069 John **Gordon**
Corporal S/7604551 Trevor **Gorman**
Private S/109062 Alexander Thomas **Graham**
Private T/58085 William **Graham**
Private S/147451 Forbes **Grant**
Warrant Officer Class II Roy **Grant**
Private 158018 Harold Ernest **Graves**

Private S/128803 Silas Anthony **Greenfield**
Private S/97531 James **Grice**
Private S/52034 Edwin **Griffiths**
Warrant Officer Class II Francis Henry **Grinnall**
Lance Corporal T/60452 Walter Frederick **Haines**
Private S/147280 Frederick John **Harris**
Private S/158344 Gerald Egerton **Harris**
Private S/98870 Harold **Harris**
Private 147815 Sidney **Harrison**
Driver T/120291 William **Harrison**
Driver T/5724429 Richard Harry **Harvey**
Private S/147864 Frank **Headland**
Driver T/81722 David **Herbert**
Private S/49460 Joseph Walter **Hickling**
Sergeant T/3300699 George William **Hill**
Driver 312126 Walter Bertram **Hodgekinson**
Private S/4803846 Arthur **Holland**
Private S/94990 Edward James **Holmes**
Private T/74668 Harold Atkin **Holt**
Corporal S/5876 George William **Hopkins**
Corporal S/94761 Arthur George **How**
Private 105540 John Oliver **Hughes**
Private 136004 George Dory **Humphreys**
Private S/114695 Lewis Vincent **Hunt**
Private S/54649 William **Hunter**
Private 830657 Reginald **Hurley**
Private S/161335 Alfred Frederick James **Ingram**
Private T/98927 Reginald Frederick **Isger**
Private S/147734 Thomas Joseph **Jamison**
Corporal T/5932 Reginald Solomon **Jefferies**
Warrant Officer Class II S/54601 William Rees **Jenkins**
Private S/98267 Wilfred Edmund **Johnson**

Driver T/58405 George Frank **Johnstone**
Private S/2756655 John Robertson **Johnstone**
Sergeant T/4186951 David Meirion **Jones**
Corporal S/9333 Ernest **Jones**
Corporal T/150007 Evan Dilwyn Charles **Jones**
Private 98945 Lewis Ernest Hugh **Jones**
Private S/114677 Tom W **Jones**
Private S/153717 Hugh **Kearney**
Private S/105471 Francis **Kelgy**
Driver T/72226 Francis Leslie **Kennard**
Corporal 94049 John William Charles **Kenton**
Corporal S/54127 John Clifford **Kerry**
Driver T/44567 Charles James **Keywood**
Private S/52692 John **Kinsey**
Lieutenant 113813 Walter Morris **Kirkham**
Private S/147907 Albert **Knight**
Private 163195 Allan **Larkin**
Private 5952096 Charles Sidney **Lawman**
Private S/137045 Arthur **Leishman**
Corporal 148780 Cecil Sheridan **Lewis**
Private S/7604555 William Trevor **Lewis**
Private T/98980 Frank **Lightbown**
Lieutenant 118257 Alfred Douglas **Lloyd**
Driver 99019 Donald Gunn **Macleod**
Corporal S/54140 Ernest George **Manning**
Sergeant S/94330 David Charles James **Matthews**
Private S/127363 Francis **McGee**
Private 99020 Donald **McMillan**
Private 105151 Thomas Alexander **McMurray**
Private T/70305 George **McVie**
Private S/98256 John Thomas **Meddle**
Private S/152598 James Kenneth **Mills**

Lance Corporal T/74384 John Cecil **Mills**
Driver T/49747 Frederick William **Mison**
Private S/147721 David John **Morgan**
Lance Corporal 6457118 Vincent **Morgan**
Driver T/53753 Cecil Harry **Moore**
Private S/57306 Sydney Ernest **Moore**
Private T/50522 Alfred David **Morris**
Private 147519 Arthur Leonard **Morris**
Corporal 148152 Hartley Kirby **Morris**
Private T/127367 Charles **Munnerley**
Driver T/153057 Donald Ernest **Naylor**
Private S/147653 Charles **Newbon**
Corporal S/148584 Joseph **Novis**
Driver 71268 Allan Edward **Nutton**
Sergeant 148809 Arthur Robert **Oakfield**
Lance Corporal T/63410 Robert **Orr**
Sergeant S/52283 Robert **Parker**
Private T/104178 Willis Roy **Parker**
Driver T/133468 Dennis Frederick **Parks**
Private T/109755 Noel **Parry**
Private S/934505 Victor Roye **Parsons**
Private T/153057 Ronald Charles **Pates**
Private 147707 Gavin Browning **Paton**
Driver T/33960 Leonard **Peek**
Corporal S/148531 Edward **Penfold**
Driver T/114027 Arnold **Pennington**
Lance Corporal T/63441 George Ernest Ward **Penny**
Warrant Officer Class II S/105535 Edward **Perkins**
Sergeant S/147854 Ernest Edward **Pilgrim**
Private S/147042 Edward Victor **Pinchon**
Driver T/158079 Edward Harold **Pitson**
Private T/109856 George Forster **Place**

Private T/146558 Robert Frederick **Potter**
Driver T/125462 Thomas William **Powell**
Private S/97605 Trevor Glyn **Price**
Driver T/125459 William **Price**
Warrant Officer Class II Fred James Ronald **Puddicombe**
Private T/73927 Arthur Ernest **Ratcliff**
Driver T/63985 Harry William **Read**
Private 105370 Arthur James **Reed**
Private T/104051 Michael James **Reed**
Private 94242 William Maxwell **Renner**
Private S/90419 Andrew Turnbull **Richardson**
Corporal S/54511 Alfred Hedley **Ridley**
Private S/74338 William John **Rigler**
Private 121658 William John **Rodger**
Corporal T/99956 Thomas Henry **Rodgers**
Sergeant S/37833 Herbert Edward **Rowe**
Private S/115221 Raymond Arnold **Salloway**
Corporal S/94027 Charles Herbert **Scott**
Lance Corporal S/100772 Frank **Shaw**
Private T/63055 Joseph Heath **Sherlock**
Lance Corporal T/64474 Ralph William John **Shotter**
Private T/48038 John **Short**
Driver T/137854 John Henry **Short**
Driver T/71115 Roland Edmund **Slade**
Private 99772 Harry Norman **Smallman**
Private S/93011 Arthur **Smith**
Private 147498 Reginald Clifford Edwin **Smith**
Driver T/104370 Walter James **Smith**
Private S/114034 Francis Percy **Spooner**
Lance Corporal S/11824 Robert **Stevens**
Private T/53609 Thomas James **Stewart**
Private T/136019 William **Stewart**

Driver T/161023 Robert Henry **Street**
Private S/10516 Cyril Thomas **Sutton**
Lance Corporal T/3770619 Joseph Herbert **Tate**
Driver 99997 Albert **Taylor**
Lance Corporal 73997 John Samuel **Taylor**
Private S/159121 Thomas Turnbull **Temple**
Corporal T/53773 Tom Smith **Thomas**
Corporal S/4912570 Albert W **Thompson**
Private 17027 James **Thompson**
Private S/52590 James William **Thorley**
Sergeant S/880834 Frederick Albert **Timms**
Lance Corporal T/5766793 William Charles **Tooke**
Private S/148889 Joseph **Tracey**
Corporal 6457199 Cecil John Leonard **Tucker**
Corporal T/36856 George Henry **Turner**
Corporal S/94401 William **Vass**
Sergeant S/94220 Charles Edward **Vidler**
Private S/11982 James Leslie **Wallwin**
Driver T/127304 Simon Christopher **Walsh**
Private T/53610 Thomas Gordon **Walters**
Private S/148726 Albert Cecil **Warwick**
Driver T/7875947 Albert Thomas **Watkins**
Private S/105697 Thomas **Watson**
Private S/147410 Alfred Charles **Webb**
Private S/5721218 Harold Mathew **White**
Warrant Officer Class II 94924 Patrick Godlovton **White**
Private 148734 Henry Raymond **Wigley**
Corporal S/94105 William George **Wilkins**
Private S/94386 Albert Edward **Willcock**
Private S/135979 Harold **Williams**
Private S/147603 Charles Albert **Woods**
Private S/105368 John Hewitt **Worrall**

Lance Corporal S/934599 Charles Richard **Wright**
Private S/6344381 Arthur **Young**
Sergeant 147889 Victor Irving **Zapp**

Royal Army Ordnance Corps

Private 7594089 Alexander Gray **Adams**
Private 7622115 Ernest Emanuel Stone **Aldred**
Private 7593143 Arthur Gordon **Alexander**
Private 7603156 John **Ashcroft**
Private 7610715 Sidney **Bell**
Private 7603738 Arthur Percival **Bignall**
Private 7612410 Reginald **Bradshaw**
Private 7594680 Cyril Herbert **Caddy**
Private 7619679 John **Cairns**
Private 7607366 Alfred **Champion**
Private 7624737 Harold Edwin **Clarke**
Private 7593720 Frank **Colbridge**
Private 7616539 Francis **Corbett**
Private 7594509 Cecil Charles **Cox**
Private 7611778 Reginald Edward **Crips**
Captain 120327 Goodwin Julian **Davis**
Private 7605198 Stephen **Dickens**
Private 7589067 Joseph William Patrick **Diviani**
Lance Corporal 7611733 William James **Douglas**
Private 7621647 William Frederick **Draper**
Private 7593501 Donald Walter **Dutson**
Private 7625084 Richard **Dwyer**
Private 7607390 Harold Weir **Eddy**
Lance Corporal 7593660 Cyril **Emsell**
Private 5943268 William **Field**
Lance Corporal 7593606 Dennis Erktwald **Forshaw**
Private 7593913 Francis Victor **Fuller**

Private 7616967 Joseph **Gaskell**
Private 7617144 Eric **Green**
Private 7612364 Peter John **Hale**
Private 7594020 Hugh Stanley **Hancock**
Private 7623949 Cuthbert Dennis **Hanson**
Warrant Officer Class I 7582340 William John **Harrison**
Private 7589208 James Naylor **Healey**
Private 7593299 Alfred Charles William **Hellyer**
Private 7594369 Harry James **Henson**
Corporal 7605366 Albert Ernest **Hicks**
Private 7586426 Lambert William **Hood**
Private 7613411 John Edward **Inman**
Private 7624263 Thomas William **Jackson**
Private 7616143 William Frederick **Jacobs**
Corporal 7583809 Leonard William **Johnson**
Private 7603652 Walter **Johnston**
Private 7593967 Eric Sydney Rolston **Jones**
Private 7593679 Kenneth Lewis **Jones**
Private 594116 Robert Denham **Jones**
Sergeant 7613310 Joseph **Jump**
Private 7624270 Edgar William **Kent**
Private 7623981 John Frederick **King**
Private 7594035 John Stephen **Lamb**
Lance Corporal 7610401 George Henry **Lee**
Private 7594242 William **Lillico**
Lance Corporal 7593810 Alexander **Loudon**
Private 7593789 Ian Francis **Macleod**
Lance Corporal 851738 George Alfred **Marsh**
Lance Corporal 7593681 Cyril Arthur **Marshall**
Lance Corporal 7589191 John **Marshall**
Private 7613358 Charles **Maylor**
Private 7593725 James **McKee**

Private 7612303 William Bennie **McLuckie**

Lance Corporal 7680165 Thomas **McNally**

Private 7869653 William James **Middleton**

Private 7603217 David **Miller**

Corporal 7613317 Samuel Philip **Mitchell**

Private 7603207 Andrew Walker **Mouat**

Private 7612934 Robert **Moyle**

Private 6463478 Leonard Frederick **Murray**

Private 7586402 Harold Vincent **Parker**

Private 7593914 Charles Henry **Pepperell**

Private 7594090 Reginald John **Phillips**

Private 7620739 George **Pickstock**

Lance Corporal 7613382 Arthur **Pickup**

Private 7594346 Charles **Price**

Sergeant 7591313 Peter Basil **Priddey**

Lance Corporal 3527803 Albert Joseph **Probert**

Private 7612531 Leslie John **Richards**

Private 7613957 Robert Dennis **Richards**

Private 7604032 William John **Richards**

Private 3591571 William Hensley **Richardson**

Private 7611557 Arthur Cecil **Rhodes**

Lance Corporal 7595973 Douglas Eric **Rumsby**

Private 7586299 Henry John **Sawyer**

Private 7612698 George **Simmonds**

Private 7618593 Edward Jeremiah **Smith**

Private 7620328 Henry Radford **Spencer**

Private 50441 John Henry **Stafford**

Lance Sergeant 4968434 George Henry **Swinn**

Private 7593554 Geoffrey Bavin **Taylor**

Private 7594156 John Colin **Thomas**

Private 7593462 Percy Reginald **Thomas**

Private 7624821 William Arnold **Thompson**

Private 7593570 Percy Norman **Townsend**
Sergeant 7605139 Hubert Lorimer **Trill**
Private 7589108 Francis Leonard **Truscott**
Private 7601686 Ernest **Turner**
Private 2978605 Andrew Sutherland **Queen**
Private 7593614 Fred **Wadsworth**
Private 7609845 Haydn **Walker**
Lance Corporal 7593560 Robert William **Wall**
Lieutenant 127985 Harry James **Ward**
Private 7610835 Martin Ernest John **Westmorland**
Corporal 7613390 Milton **White**
Warrant Officer Class II Philip **Whitehead**
Private 7594472 George Ambrose **Wickham**
Private 7593889 Charles Morgan **Wilmot**
Private 7624595 Sydney George **Wright**
Private 7603738 Frederick Thomas **Wynne**
Private 7612237 William Smith **Yates**
Sergeant 7612206 John Railton **Yielder**

Royal Engineers

Sapper 1913367 John Henry **Adams**
Sapper 1902499 William George **Adams**
Sapper 1892866 John **Akeroyd**
Sapper 1910047 Harold **Alcock**
Lance Corporal 2189400 Sidney Flowett **Alderson**
Sapper 1913266 Colin Henry James **Aldom**
Sapper 1910525 Arthur Vernon **Aldred**
Lance Corporal 1867988 Robert **Allen**
Sapper 1880397 Henry **Anderton**
Sapper 1914278 Harold Frederick **Aplin**
Lance Sergeant 1828802 Herbert John Charles James **Apps**
Sapper 1880572 Joseph Cuthbert **Atherton**

Sapper 2193864 Donald **Atkinson**

Corporal 2030311 Horace Ernest **Ayears**

Sapper 5495828 Albert Sydney **Baker**

Sapper 1505919 Kenneth Arthur **Balls**

Sapper 1911259 Kenneth Lawrence **Barnard**

Driver 1884183 Norman Alfred **Barrick**

Lance Corporal 1899079 David Kerr **Barrie**

Sapper 1903464 William Frederick **Barron**

Sapper 1903465 Frederick William George **Barton**

Sapper 1887433 Lewis Stevenson **Barty**

Staff Sergeant 1868848 Harry James **Bateman**

Sapper 1926144 Ernest William **Bayliss**

Lance Corporal 777043 Frederick William **Beames**

Sapper 1903410 John Hardy **Bean**

Driver 1882312 John **Bell**

Sapper 1914607 John Edward Scott **Bell**

Warrant Officer Class II 1863807 Frederick John **Bennett**

Lance Sergeant 7607645 Henry James **Bennett**

Sapper 1926501 Arthur George **Betteridge**

Sapper 1912389 Charles Edward **Bird**

Sapper 1913351 Lawrence William **Bird**

Sapper 2187336 Bernard Richard **Black**

Sapper 1891863 Charles **Black**

Sapper 2079626 Horace Walter **Blackman**

Sapper 1904631 Albert **Blakely**

Sapper 1879391 Stanley Charles **Bott**

Sapper 1889970 Wilfred **Bourne**

Lieutenant 126096 Charles Edward **Bowdidge**

Sapper 1911508 John William **Bowen**

Captain 120002 William **Bowles**

Sapper 1927307 John **Breeze**

Sapper 19143330 Lorraine Ernest Walter **Brind**

Lance Sergeant 311142 Frederick George **Britt**
Sapper 1875389 Edward Arthur **Bromfield**
Sapper 1985633 James **Brotherton**
Lance Corporal 2067340 Eric George **Brown**
Lance Corporal 1917041 Herbert **Brown**
Sapper 1887700 James Buchan **Brown**
Sapper 1899084 James Paton **Bryan**
Sapper 1905283 Eric **Buckley**
Captain 107035 Harold **Burleigh**
Sapper 1986624 Harry **Butterworth**
Sapper 1880214 John Anthony **Byrne**
Sapper 1899148 Edwin **Calvert**
Corporal 2189402 Ernest **Calvert**
Lance Corporal 1899093 Peter Paterson **Cameron**
Lance Corporal 1899086 James **Campbell**
Sapper 1914062 Horace Fredrick Hugh **Cannell**
Sapper 3518207 Daniel **Casson**
Sapper 1913126 Charles **Chalmers**
Sapper 1891908 John Alfred **Chambers**
Sapper 2189387 Wilfred **Cheetham**
Sapper 4973924 Samuel Walter **Clarke**
Lance Corporal 2193464 Donald **Clay**
Sapper 1882256 William John **Coats**
Sergeant 2717668 Michael **Coffey**
Sapper 1927431 Albert Frederick **Coles**
Corporal 1918148 James Richard **Colquitt**
Sapper 1918032 Frederick **Copsey**
Sapper 1914323 Arthur **Cour**
Sapper 1904286 Percy **Cowin**
Sergeant 1867969 Richard Godfrey **Coxhead**
Sapper 1887420 Harold **Cracknell**
Sapper 2186735 Godfrey **Craggs**

Sapper 18981849 Herbert **Cuncliffe**

Sapper 1883072 Ray **Darby**

Sapper 1927325 George James **Davey**

Sergeant 1870057 Eric **Day**

Sapper 1899035 Arthur **Deacon**

Sapper 3528225 Harry Sydney **Deacon**

Lance Corporal 3949440 Alfred **Derrick**

Sapper 1899133 Duncan **Dick**

Sapper 1917143 William Jackson **Doherty**

Sapper 1908941 Ernest Charles **Donovan**

Sergeant 1867367 Frank **Dowling**

Sapper 1854359 Albert James **Dowse**

Corporal 3522745 William Austin **Doyle**

Sapper 1882316 Frederick **Draper**

Sapper 1918081 Joseph **Duffy**

Sapper 1903478 Cyril **Duquemin**

Lance Corporal 2193222 Harold **Edwards**

Sapper 1927417 William John **Elward**

Sapper 5382598 Charles Arthur **Essen**

Sapper 3132238 James **Etheridge**

Sapper 4194872 Percy Llewellyn Leonard **Evans**

Sapper 1903432 William Henry **Evans**

Sapper 1892864 William **Faragher**

Sapper 1912306 Francis Robert **Farline**

Sapper 1898823 Arthur **Farrall**

Lance Sergeant 1927191 Richard Reuben **Fellender**

Corporal 2187338 Arthur **Fenwick**

Sapper 1891796 Walter **Fielding**

Sapper 1903520 Albert William **Filmer**

Sapper 4384911 Stanley Latchwood **Fitch**

Sergeant 1866342 George **Fitzpatrick**

Sapper 1918047 George **Flemming**

Lance Corporal 1892938 Frederick Edward **Fletcher**
Lance Corporal 2313455 Walter Sydney **Frostick**
Sapper 1923629 William Frederick **Fuggle**
Lance Corporal 1872703 Fred **Fryer**
Sapper 2193850 William **Gibbins**
Sapper 1904515 Leonard **Gibbs**
Corporal 2573023 Henry William **Gibson**
Sapper 1889874 Joseph Edwin **Ginns**
Sapper 1927439 Joseph Ivor **Goode**
Lance Corporal 1881687 Francis Gerard **Goudy**
Lance Sergeant 1904582 George Henry **Gray**
Sapper 1892877 Frederick William **Green**
Lance Corporal 1904568 Albert **Greenhill**
Sapper 1911237 Montague Raymond **Griffin**
Sapper 1898735 Harold Edward **Griffiths**
Driver 2189393 George Frederick **Grimshaw**
Sapper 869109 Arthur W **Grocock**
Sapper 1910375 William Alfred **Haigh**
Sapper 1848828 Joseph George **Hailstone**
Sapper 1880671 Cecil Pinnington **Hall**
Sapper 1882253 Cyril Robert **Halliday**
Sapper 1914224 Thomas George **Hamper**
Sapper 1898654 Trevor Haig **Harris**
Sapper 1980425 William James **Harris**
Sapper 1917091 Albert **Hart**
Sapper 189958 Edwin Albert **Hartigan**
Sapper 5565591 Thomas Henry **Hassell**
Sapper 1892998 Ronald **Hathway**
Sapper 1912487 George Edward **Hay**
2nd Lieutenant 120577 William Edward **Hayward**
Sapper 1904268 John Charles **Hennah**
Driver 1884175 Frederick Jeffrey James **Herman**

Sapper 1913129 Charles **Heron**
Corporal 2021129 Alfred Edward **Heskins**
Sapper 2193201 Eric Tennison **Hill**
Sapper 1909657 Thomas William **Hill**
Sapper 1912462 Norman Harry **Hiscock**
Sapper 1903357 Albert **Holliday**
Sapper 1902517 John **Hood**
Sapper 1914279 John Eden **Horton**
Sapper 1902521 Thomas **Howard**
Sapper 2189413 Tom **Howcroft**
Sapper 2189411 George **Hudson**
2nd Lieutenant 100608 James Hubert **Hughes**
Sapper 2186736 Ernest **Hullah**
Sapper 1917049 Henry **Hunt**
Lance Corporal 1927376 Norman **Husselbee**
Sapper 1911260 Frederick Ernest **Inkpen**
Sapper 1902675 Henry Arthur **Ireton**
Sapper 809775 Stanley Arthur **James**
Sapper 1927266 John **John**
Driver 1884182 Ernest Victor **Johnson**
Driver 1913414 Robert **Johnson**
Sapper 5333719 James Henry **Jones**
Corporal 802912 Talieson **Jones**
Sapper 1987233 Hubert James **King**
Sapper 1914308 George Richard **Kingsman**
Sapper 1898241 Wilfred Henry **Knibb**
Sapper 4530328 Alfred **Lazenby**
Sapper 1912429 Sydney **Lea**
Sapper 5490408 William **Ledger**
Sapper 1887884 Stanley Louis **Letch**
Lance Corporal 1911276 Horace **Lewis**
Sapper 1898023 Alun Rees **Lloyd**

Driver 2184641 Harold **Lobley**
Lance Corporal 4441190 Thomas Curry **Lovett**
Sapper 1903526 Thomas **Maguire**
Lance Corporal 2189416 Luke **Marson**
Sapper 1889532 Albert Reginald **Martin**
Sapper 1913115 Harold Samuel **Mayer**
Sapper 1899083 James **McDougall**
Sapper 1913130 Archibald Burgess **McIntyre**
Sapper 2079112 Thomas **McIntyre**
Sergeant 2923178 Angus **McKinnon**
Sapper 1912461 Douglas Herbert **Michell**
Sapper 1898460 Lloyd Herbert **Mills**
Sapper 1882097 Charles John **Mudge**
Sapper 2064323 Charles William **Muller**
Sapper 1899076 James Kerr **Murray**
Sapper 1913127 James Strachan **Murray**
Sapper 1899067 James **Newsham**
Sapper 1901882 George William **Nichol**
Lance Corporal 1894080 Cyril **Nicholls**
Sapper 1899072 John **O'Neil**
Sapper 1913322 Thomas **Orme**
Sapper 4857083 Frank **Orton**
Sapper 1891810 Clifford **Owen**
Lance Corporal 2075951 Douglas Frank **Owen**
Sapper 3514516 Ambrose Maurice **Paltridge**
Sapper 2183817 Harry **Parkinson**
Sapper 1899069 John Rogerson **Parrington**
Sapper 1901404 Osborne Charles **Parry**
Sapper 1898948 Sidney Thomas **Payton**
Sapper1891958 Gervase Robert **Phillips**
Lance Corporal 1894169 Joseph **Pitcher**
Lance Corporal 2036306 Ernest Edward **Plummer**

Sapper 1041271 Ralph Frederick **Pond**
Sapper 1923011 John **Potter**
Sapper 1892994 James Wilson **Powell**
Sapper 1898067 Victor George **Powell**
Sapper 1898382 Douglas Harry **Prince**
Sapper 1914322 Joseph Edward **Raddings**
Sapper 1913181 Albert Marshall **Ramsay**
Sapper 1913102 Frederick Charles **Rastall**
Sapper 1892992 Clifford **Rawle**
Lance Corporal 1055118 Arthur **Rayner**
Sapper 1898525 Christopher **Reader**
Corporal 1904428 Charles **Reeve**
Sapper 1914381 Geoffrey **Richardson**
Sapper 2047649 William **Robinson**
Sapper 1907341 Frank Stanley **Rowe**
Lance Corporal 1902498 Reginald Clifford **Rowe**
Driver 1878857 William **Rowe**
Sapper 1898906 Henry Albert **Rowley**
Sapper 2067518 Sydney James **Ruck**
Corporal 2189404 Charles Frederick **Sanderson**
Sapper 1874916 Terence John **Schlesinger**
Sapper 2189397 George **Scott**
Lance Corporal 1915180 Percy **Scott**
Lance Corporal 1875632 William Robert Peter **Shadwick**
Sapper 2207307 William John **Shannon**
Sapper 3599756 Victor **Shaw**
Sapper 1898164 Stephen Tom **Shearing**
Lance Sergeant 1873141 Frank James **Shears**
Sapper 1908948 Stanley George **Shepherd**
Sapper 1882257 William Charles **Shepherd**
Lance Corporal 1982775 Ernest Percy **Shute**
Driver 2183819 Thomas Henry **Siberry**

Sapper 1911263 Ronald Arthur **Silver**

Sapper 1917064 George Albert **Silvey**

Sapper 2186742 Edwin **Skaife**

Sapper 1907459 Douglas **Smith**

Driver 1884207 Duglass Frank **Smith**

Sapper 1911362 Hector Thomas **Smith**

Sapper 835946 Frederick Alan **Spencer**

Sapper 1918055 Albert Henry Caistor **Staniland**

Sapper 1911265 James **Sugrue**

Sapper 1899147 Harold **Taylor**

Sapper 1927008 Brinley Clifford **Thomas**

Sapper 1899075 James **Thornton**

Sapper 1902527 Harold D **Thorpe**

Sapper 1882243 Richard George **Tonkin**

Sapper 1007874 Harold **Towell**

Corporal 1869351 James **Tremlow**

Lance Sergeant 1983641 Reginald Robert **Tucker**

2nd Lieutenant 115439 Frank Eardley **Turner**

Sapper 1914201 George Frederick **Turner**

Sergeant 1902520 Walter **Unsworth**

Sapper 1891912 James Maitland **Walker**

Sapper 18877585 Leslie **Walker**

Sapper 1869996 Thomas **Walker**

Sapper 1906567 John Harry **Wallace**

Sapper 3380854 William **Walsh**

Sapper 1909662 Clifford **Walters**

Sapper 1987197 Horace **Warboys**

Sapper 1928050 Henry Aidan **Ward**

Captain 104659 Edward Allan **Warren**

Sapper 1907557 George Moses **Watling**

Sapper 2194547 Harold **Webb**

Warrant Officer Class 1 William **West**
Sapper 1922558 Thomas Henry **White**
Lieutenant Colonel 9079 Berkeley Frederic **Whitestone**
Sapper 1901792 Christian Ronald **Wickert**
Sapper 1912465 Eric Cecil **Wilkin**
Sergeant 1853873 Ernest George **Williams**
Sapper 1870080 Francis Herbert **Williams**
Sapper 1901134 Thomas Francis **Williams**
Sapper 1927174 William John **Williams**
Sapper 1927338 Walter Leslie **Woodward**
Sapper 2189406 Douglas **Wright**
Drive 2189389 George Herbert **Wright**
Lance Corporal 6077 834 Frederick Leonard **Wyber**
Sapper 1903296 Albert Henry **Yates**

Some forty different military units including the RAF, Merchant Navy, Corps and Regiments, lost men as a result of the sinking of the *Lancastria*. For some, it was the single largest number of men they lost throughout the entire seven years of the war.

The RAF had approximately 800 personnel on board the *Lancastria*, most of whom were support staff, such as mechanics, rather than pilots. They were together inside the ship's number two hold, which was where one of the three bombs that struck the ship, exploded. The damage sustained as a result of the subsequent explosions, caused her to list and sink within just twenty minutes. Those on board the stricken vessel, who hadn't been trapped below decks, and made good their escape, had the added danger of having to dive into, and swim through the estimated 1,400 tons of fuel that had leaked from the ship. If that had ignited and set off an explosion, it is highly unlikely that there would have been any survivors at all.

A number of the civilians on board were the wives and children of British military personnel, but many of them were French refugees, trying their best to escape the advancing German army that was rapidly making its way to the French coast.

CHAPTER 11

HMT *Lancastria* – The Aftermath

There were many battles, operations and incidents during the Second World War that were deserving of special recognition, but none were ever issued with their own official medal, that is except for the sinking of the HMT *Lancastria*. There are those who would question the issue of such an award when events such as the D-Day Normandy landings, the evacuations at Dunkirk, the Battle of Britain and the Blitz, to name just a few, did not receive any such similar official recognition, other than the gratitude of a grateful nation.

The British government never saw fit to issue such an award, but the Scottish government did and commissioned a medal in 2008, with survivors and relatives of those lost, having up until 15 May 2015 to apply for one.

I had always wondered why the Scottish government had decided to issue a medal. Was it because the number of Scottish military servicemen lost in the tragedy is estimated to have been in the region of about 400? Was it because the *Lancastria,* initially named the RMS *Tyrrhenia,* was built in 1920 by William Beardmore and Company, a Scottish engineering and ship building company on the River Clyde, for the Anchor Line, a subsidiary of the Cunard Line?

It is quite remarkable that the sinking of the *Lancastria* is still remembered and commemorated so passionately to this day. The HMT *Lancastria* Association, which had previously been in existence as the *Lancastria* Survivors Association, founded by Major Peter Petit, still hold a remembrance service at the Church of St Katharine Cree in the City of London. The church was founded in 1280, with the present building dating from 1630. It can be found on the north side of Leadenhall Street, in the ward of Aldgate, and is one of the buildings that survived the Great Fire of London in 1666.

The *Lancastria* Association of Scotland was formed much later in 2005. It also holds an annual remembrance service which is held at St George's West Church in Edinburgh, which is the largest memorial service held in the UK and regularly has representatives from both the Scottish and French governments in attendance. Work on the building was completed in 1784. Their annual service is held on the closest Saturday to 17 June each year.

In 2015 Veteran's Secretary, Keith Brown, said the Scottish government had commissioned a medal for the *Lancastria* survivors and the relatives of those who were killed, because:

> *We in Scotland feel a strong bond with the servicemen and women who have served us throughout the years and continue to protect the democratic freedoms we still enjoy today.*

The commemorative HMS Lancastria *medal from the Scottish government is a lasting reminder of our gratitude to those who made the ultimate sacrifice on that fateful day. Their memory is honoured, their place in history is secured.*

The medal was designed by the grandson of Walter Hirst, a survivor of the sinking, and includes an inscription on the rear:

In recognition of the ultimate sacrifice of the 4000 victims of Britain's worst ever maritime disaster and the endurance of survivors. We will remember them.

The front of the medal includes the words: *HMT Lancastria – 17th June 1940.*

On 17 June 2015, the occasion of the 75th anniversary of the sinking of the *Lancastria*, the then Chancellor of the Exchequer, George Osborne MP, who in the absence of the Prime Minister, David Cameron, made reference to the loss of the *Lancastria* at Prime Minister's Questions, in the House of Commons said:

It was kept secret at the time for reasons of wartime secrecy, but I think it is appropriate today in this House of Commons to remember all those who died, those who survived, and those who mourn.

The reason Winston Churchill gave in his memoirs about why he initially wanted to keep the sinking of the *Lancastria* under wraps, was so as not unduly affect the morale of the British people, who he said, had already had to endure too much in the way of loss and defeat. The D-Notice he had put in place to prevent the Press from reporting on the sinking, lasted just five weeks before it was written about – initially in America on 25 July 1940, and thereafter throughout the pages of numerous British newspapers.

There are numerous memorials to those who lost their lives in the sinking of the *Lancastria*, on both sides of the English Channel. British military personnel, the names of those who were lost in the disaster appeared on memorials in different locations, depending on which service they were in. For example, soldiers who were part of the British Expeditionary Force, but whose bodies were never found, have their names commemorated on the Dunkirk Memorial. Those with naval connections are similarly commemorated on the naval memorials at Chatham, Plymouth and Portsmouth. Those who served with the Merchant Navy are remembered at the Tower Hill Memorial, whilst members of the Royal Air Force are included on the Runnymede Memorial at Englefield Green near Egham in Surrey.

There is a memorial on the sea front at St Nazaire in France which has the following inscription.

In proud memory of more than 4,000 who died and in commemoration of the people of Saint Nazaire and surrounding districts who saved many lives, tended wounded and gave a Christian burial to victims.

St Katharine Cree church in the City of London where the *Lancastria* annual memorial service is held, is also the final resting place of the ship's bell. There are at least five other different memorials that directly relate to the loss of the *Lancastria* and those who were the victims of her sinking.

The wreck site of the *Lancastria* is in French territorial waters, and therefore cannot be covered under the British Protection of Military Remains Act 1986. In 2006 the French government gave the *Lancastria* wreck site legal protection as a war grave.

There is no way of knowing for certain how many men, women and children were lost with the sinking of the *Lancastria*, but undoubtedly for those who were stuck inside her before she went down, it will have been their final resting place. As a designated war grave the lost souls of those who died that day will now be left to rest in peace for ever more.

On Saturday 3 August 1940, just six weeks after the sinking of the *Lancastria*, a wedding took place at the St James's Episcopal Church in Aberdeen, Scotland. What connected the event to the disaster of 17 June 1940 was the fact that bridegroom and a number of the survivors were among the guests.

The bridegroom was Major H.E. Seymour-Thomas, of the Auxiliary Military Pioneer Corps, and the bride was Sister Ruth Dyke, who was a nurse in a hospital at Dieppe. The hospital was bombed and resulted in Sister Dyke and her colleagues being evacuated from France as part of Operation Aerial.

Major Seymour-Thomas was also stationed in Dieppe and served with a Pioneer Company. He was amongst one of the last to be evacuated from Dieppe, and along with his men, had to walk the entire distance to St Nazaire.

Once there they were taken out to the *Lancastria* by a tug boat, which was lying some 5 miles off shore. By way of coincidence, the boat behind Major Seymour-Thomas's, included Major the Reverend W.R. Torvaney MC, who performed the couple's marriage service. As if by some heavenly intervention, the reverend's boat, which had initially attempted to unload those on board on to the *Lancastria*, was turned away and directed to another vessel, as by then it could not take any more people.

Also amongst those who were taken aboard the *Lancastria,* was Lieutenant R. Haynes, a fellow officer of the bridegroom, who gave the bride away at the wedding. She wore a two-piece suit of dusty pink angora and a wine-coloured silk turban trimmed with veiling. Her accessories matched her hat and a spray of orchids was pinned at the neckline of her dress.

When the bride and bridegroom left the church they were greeted by a guard of honour who performed an archway with their spades. In command of the guard of honour were Company Sergeant Major Tasker and Company Quartermaster Sergeant Major Burton, who were with Major Seymour-Thomas in France, and who were also saved from the *Lancastria* disaster, as were several of the men who formed the honour guard.

There were many deeds of gallantry and, terrible though the experience was, there were many moments of humour, shared by those present. Major Torvaney was keen to pay tribute to the men aboard the small French boats in the bay off St Nazaire, who did a lot of the conveying back to shore of British soldiers from the *Lancastria* who had jumped into the sea before it sank.

They did this without being asked or instructed to do so and despite the obvious dangers to themselves.

Just three weeks later on Saturday 24 August 1940, another wedding took place at the same church, with the ceremony being performed by the same priest who had married Major Seymour-Thomas and his bride.   On this occasion it was the turn of Sergeant John King, another member of the Auxiliary Military Pioneer Corps, a fellow survivor of the sinking of the *Lancastria*, and a man who served under Major Seymour-Thomas in France.

Sergeant King married Miss Lily McKenzie Coutts, the daughter of Mrs Stuart, of 14 Kidd Street, Aberdeen. The bride was given away by Company Quartermaster Sergeant Burton, also a member of the Pioneer Corps, whilst Company Sergeant Major Tasker MM was the best man.

Sergeant Downing MM, Sergeant Duckworth and Sergeant Dyoss, all serving members of the Auxiliary Military Pioneer Corps who had been in France as part of the British Expeditionary Force, along with a number of sergeants from the Royal Engineers, formed a guard of honour as the bride and groom left the church. Amongst those present were Lieutenant Proudfoot and Lieutenant Haynes, the latter had given away the bride at the wedding of Lieutenant Seymour-Thomas. Whilst serving in France Lieutenant Haynes had earned the nickname amongst the men of, 'Hell for leather Haynes'. After the ceremony a reception was held in the sergeants' mess of the Auxiliary Military Pioneer Corps.

On Tuesday 8 October 1940, it was announced in the *London Gazette* that a number of officers and crew of the

Lancastria, had been awarded medals for their bravery and gallant conduct during the disaster of 17 June 1940.

The ship's Captain, Rudolph Sharp, the Chief Officer, Harry Grattidge, along with the Chief Engineer, were all awarded the Officer of the British Empire (OBE), Civil Division as were the ship's Chief Steward, Frederick Entwistle Beattie; David Irvine Jardine Thomson, the ship's boatswain mate, and William Herbert Stone, the ship's gunner.

Commended for their conduct and bravery were, Richard Goranway, the senior first officer, who was killed in the tragedy, Wilfred John Hyde, a senior assistant purser, James Duncan, senior second engineer, Arthur Dover, extra second steward, Michael Murphy, the quartermaster and the ship's surgeon, John Hill, who was also killed.

On Friday, 14 September 1945, it was announced that Private Donald Tidmarsh of the 1st/5th Battalion, Sherwood Foresters, had been released from his captivity in a prisoner of war camp in Osaka, Japan, and was 'safely back in Allied hands'.

He was one of those who had survived the sinking of the *Lancastria*. In October 1941, Private Tidmarsh and his colleagues from 1st/5th Battalion, Sherwood Foresters, sailed from Liverpool on the converted P&O cruise liner, the troop ship, *Orcades,* as part of the British 18th Division, which in turn was part of 55 Brigade. After a three-month journey, which saw her sail for more than 20,000 miles, the *Orcades* arrived in Singapore on 29 January 1942, to help bolster the island's defences, just 18 days before the island was surrendered to the Japanese. Donald, having escaped from France as part of the British Expeditionary

Force, ahead of the advancing German Army, in 1940, wasn't so lucky second time around. He became one of the tens of thousands of Commonwealth soldiers who became prisoners of war of the Japanese and remained in captivity until the end of the war.

In Closing

The *Lancastria* was one of hundreds of vessels that were lost during the Second World War, both military and merchant, so one obvious question concerning the *Lancastria*, is why is there so much interest in its loss?

Doubt about the number of those who died played a part, that is certain. If we take the number 6,500 written on the clipboard of one of the ship's loading officers counting those embarking on the *Lancastria*, and seen by James Burke, as a realistic figure of those on board, then at least we have a solid basis to start with. Although it is not known if that figure included the 330 members of the ship's crew.

As a pre-war cruise-liner she had a capacity of 1,300 passengers and 300 crew, but her refit as a wartime troop ship, saw that figure raised to 2,180 passengers and 330 crew. When she was used in a similar capacity to bring evacuated troops back home from Norway earlier in the war, she managed a total of 2,653. With this in mind the *Lancastria*'s commander, Captain Sharp, informed the British military authorities that he should be able to evacuate approximately 3,000 from St Nazaire. In reply, Captain Sharp was instructed to take as many people on board as was possible to do so, 'without regard to the limits of international law'.

The *Lancastria* arrived off St Nazaire about 4am on 17 June 1940 and with embarkation continuing throughout the day, by mid-afternoon, it has been estimated that the number of those on board was between 4,000 and 9,000. But it has to be emphasised that the actual figure is unknown.

Let's take a look at what we do know. Both military personnel and civilian workers and refugees were ferried out to the *Lancastria* by a number of different vessels, including local French fishing boats, tugs, other types of craft and destroyers from the Royal Navy. We know that official figures show that 1,738 people were lost when the *Lancastria* was bombed and sunk. We also know that there were 2,477 survivors from the sinking, which gives a total figure of those accounted for, as 4,215. Going back to the figure of 6,500 seen by James Burke, although we do not know if that was the final figure for those who had embarked, that would mean that at least 2,385 perished when the *Lancastria* was sunk. Anything other than this number, is guess work.

Besides all the British military personnel, some of whom were accompanied by family members, there were also an unknown number of civilian refugees on board, most of whom were French, with some no doubt Belgian, but once again nobody knows for sure exactly how many. The other point to consider is that every member of the British and Commonwealth armed forces who was killed or died during the course of the Second World War, has been accounted for and their names have been recorded and commemorated on the Commonwealth War Graves Commission records.

The other main question is did Winston Churchill and the British government try and cover up the tragedy? The answer to that is quite simply, yes. Winston Churchill instigated what was known at the time as a D-Notice to try and prevent the public hearing about the tragedy. His reason for doing so was, he said in his memoirs, to protect the public from hearing more negative news because he believed it would affect the nation's morale. That might well have been the case. Churchill had seen at first hand, how people could be affected by too much negative wartime information. It was the early setbacks which British forces had experienced in Norway and across France, which had resulted in Neville Chamberlain, effectively having to resign as Prime Minister. Churchill had witnessed this at first hand and, after finally becoming Prime Minister, he wasn't about to let the same outcome befall himself.

Maybe Churchill's decision to impose a ban on British newspapers reporting the sinking of the *Lancastria* had less to do with his worry about public morale and more to do with ensuring that he didn't have to follow in Macmillan's footsteps and resign his office.

Whatever the actual reason was, the British public and other interested parties, will not find out the truth until 2040, when the report on the sinking of the *Lancastria* is due to be released under the Official Secrets Act. To prevent the report from being released to the public for a period 100 years, strongly suggests that somebody, quite possibly Winston Churchill, had a great deal to worry about.

About the Author

Stephen is a retired Police officer having served with Essex Police as a Constable for thirty years between 1983 and 2013. Both his sons, Luke and Ross, were members of the armed forces, collectively serving five tours of Afghanistan between 2008 and 2013. Both were injured on their first tour. This led to Stephen's first book *Two Sons in a Warzone – Afghanistan: The True Story of a Father's Conflict,* which was published in October 2010.

Both of his grandfathers served in and survived the First World War, one with the Royal Irish Rifles, the other in the Merchant Navy, whilst his father served in the Royal Army Ordnance Corps during the Second World War.

Stephen corroborated with one of his writing partners, Ken Porter, on a book published in August 2012, *German POW Camp 266 – Langdon Hills,* which spent six weeks as the number one best-selling book in Waterstones, Basildon between March and April 2013. Steve and Ken collaborated on a further four books in the Towns & Cities in the Great War series by Pen and Sword. Stephen has also written other titles in the same series of books, and In February 2017 his book, *The Surrender of Singapore – Three Years of Hell 1942-45,* was published. This was followed in March 2018 by *Against All Odds: Walter Tull the Black Lieutenant,* and in January 2019, *A History of the Royal Hospital Chelsea – 1682 - 2017 – The Warrior's*

Repose, which he wrote with his wife, Tanya. They have also written two other books together.

Stephen has also co-written three crime thrillers which were published between 2010 and 2012, which centre round a fictional detective, named Terry Danvers.

When not writing, Tanya and Stephen enjoy the simplicity of walking their four German Shepherd dogs early each morning, at a time when most sensible people are still fast asleep in their beds.

Sources

Wikipedia
www.cwgc.com
www.ancestry.co.uk
www.wartimememoriesproject.com
www.militarian.com
www.britishnewspaperarchive.com
www.forces-war-records.co.uk
www.britain-at-war.org.uk

Index